Baptism of Fire

To Palena

best wishes + KEEP SAFE

regards

Geoff Bullard

BAPTISM OF FIRE

Life, Death and Piper Alpha

Geoff Bollands with Julie Gorton

Matador
9 Priory Business Park,
Wistow Road, Kibworth Beauchamp,
Leicestershire. LE8 0RX
Tel: 0116 279 2299
Email: books@troubador.co.uk
Web: www.troubador.co.uk/matador
Twitter: @matadorbooks

ISBN 978 1789013 597

British Library Cataloguing in Publication Data.
A catalogue record for this book is available from the British Library.

Printed and bound by CPI Group (UK) Ltd, Croydon, CR0 4YY
Typeset in 11pt Minion Pro by Troubador Publishing Ltd, Leicester, UK

Matador is an imprint of Troubador Publishing Ltd

I am very grateful to my family and friends who supported me during a very difficult time in my life and would like to dedicate this book to them, with a very special mention to Christine who kept the family together.

CONTENTS

Appendices:

ACKNOWLEDGEMENTS

This book would never have been written without the initial prompting and encouragement of Emmanuel Mbakwe, who was the National President of the Apostolic Church. He asked me about my experiences regarding the disaster and told me that I had a story to tell. I wasn't convinced, as a few books had already been written about the Piper Alpha disaster, the latest being *Fire in the Night* by Stephen McGinty, which presents a well-researched and excellent account.

It has been suggested at several of the presentations that I've given that I write about my experiences of the disaster from a personal point of view, recounting the sequence of events as it happened to me. It was also suggested to me that I tell my story to illustrate that, whatever difficulties we may face in life, there is always light at the end of the tunnel. The thought kept niggling away, rather like an itch that needs scratching, but I kept telling myself that I was too busy at work and I'm not a writer, I'm a Financial Adviser.

The conversation then came up with a family friend and client, Julie Gorton, who is a Librarian by profession and now lives in Suffolk. Julie was attending a writing class and offered to help and, after speaking with her, the 'itch' became something else and, with her encouragement and against my better judgement, I agreed to give it a go.

I've found the writing time-consuming at a time when I'm trying to wind down, and also very emotional and distressing at times. On occasions I've been tempted to give up and have been a little negative about the project and, without Julie's help, professional skills and encouragement, it would not have happened. All credit for this book must go to Julie; I've simply written my thoughts and Julie has organised and presented them. If you enjoy this book or get some benefit from reading it, a big thank you is down to Julie.

I would like to thank other people who have contributed to the process, to Janet Ireland for her thoughts and ideas and Angela Butler, the Office Manageress, for her proof-reading skills. Thank you to Stephen McGinty for his practical advice, help and encouragement and for writing the introduction to this book.

I thank Christine, Rachel and Hannah for their contributions, which give a very different perspective on things, and apologise for stirring up memories that they would rather forget.

Methinks that they could have been a lot more critical of me.

I will always be grateful for the men involved in rescuing and attending to us, some of whom were very brave, and in particular Brian Batchelor and Malcolm Storey who died trying to save others.

Included is a list of my former colleagues. It was a very sad day for all their families and friends.

Thank you to everyone who has put up with me throughout the writing of this book and the life recounted within it; this has been an emotional roller coaster for me. God bless you all, even if you don't believe in Him.

All pictures of the Piper Alpha Platform provided by
The Scotsman newspaper

Introduction

BY STEPHEN MCGINTY

Winston Churchill once said: 'if you're going through Hell – keep going.'
Geoff Bollands has gone through Hell and, like Winston Churchill advised,
he has managed to keep going. No one who was not present on Piper Alpha
on the evening of 6th July 1988 has any idea of what it must have been like.
Although I spent two years researching and writing my book on the disaster
Fire in the Night and a further three years developing and producing a
subsequent feature-length documentary, I would be the first to admit that
cool research is incomparable to the white hot heat of genuine experience.

Geoff Bollands lived through this terrifying experience and has now
written about it with a cool, clear detachment which gives the reader a deeper
understanding of not only what went wrong on that fateful night but what it
felt like to be in genuine fear for your life and still muster the resilience and
control to escape and assist others to do the same. Yet Geoff's book is more
than simply an account of that horrific night, for his life is so much more than
the consequences of those two tragic hours. Over the pages that follow readers
will be led by an experienced guide through the early years of the North Sea oil
exploration, what it was like to do a difficult job one enjoyed and was very good
at, and then, what it takes to turn your life around and find a new vocation.

Geoff's book not only adds to our understanding of the Piper Alpha
disaster and the off-shore world of the 1980s but gives an inspiring insight
into the resilience of the human spirit and what it takes to refuse to be
defined by the worst night of your life. Stoic, compassionate and quietly
moving, this is a book to read and, most importantly, to share.

1

A PIVOTAL DAY

Wednesday 6th July 1988 was a pivotal day in my life. I had worked the night shift in the control room on the Piper Alpha offshore oil platform in the North Sea, one hundred and thirty miles east of Aberdeen; it was my sixth shift of seven, so only one more to go before returning home to my family in Middlesbrough. Dawn broke over the platform with a light breeze that morning as my shift came to an end, the sea was calm and it promised to be a pleasant summer's day. It was a scene very far removed from that less than eighteen hours later, when gigantic fireballs would engulf the platform, causing the rig to plummet into the sea and killing one hundred and sixty-seven men[1]. Two hundred and twenty-eight men were on board.

It would be a busy day on the platform, as the midsummer months were the time when crucial maintenance, repairs and safety checks were carried out on the North Sea oil rigs. In addition, a major construction project was underway on the Piper; a new pipeline riser was being fitted on to the platform which would carry gas from the Chanter, a satellite field that had recently been discovered and assessed as a viable and profitable oil field. After a bowl of cereal, I was in bed by 6.00 am, with no inkling of the disastrous sequence of events which would unfold before my next shift later that day, leading to the worst offshore oil catastrophe the world has ever seen.

---

1   There were 228 men on Piper Alpha on 6th July 1988; 167 men died, including 2 rescue workers, and 63 survived.

I would normally go straight to bed when my shift finished at about 5.30 am, getting up at about 2.00 pm, relaxing for a while, usually by reading, before having my main meal and starting work again at 5.30 pm. The food on the rig was excellent and there was always plenty of it; I would usually have a full meal at 5.00 pm and another at the mid-shift break. The galley was open from five till seven morning and evening and eleven to one midday and midnight to accommodate the different shift patterns on the rig and there was always a full selection of food available. Most of the workers on the platform worked two shifts of 'six to six' but the drilling crews worked two shifts of 'twelve to twelve', which meant that at every meal break there were men who had just got up, men mid-shift and those who had finished their shift and were going to bed, so breakfast, lunch and dinner were always available for everybody.

The morning papers came in on the first helicopter flight of the day and those of us who worked for Occidental Petroleum had our choice of paper delivered. Having been interested in maths and finance since I was a young boy, my first choice of newspaper had been the Financial Times. However, I soon changed to the Telegraph, which also had a good financial section, when my colleagues objected, as we all read and shared each other's papers and none of them wanted to read the Financial Times. A group of us on the rig had formed a share club, which was officially registered. We contributed a set amount each month by direct debit to the club's bank account, we had regular meetings and bought and sold shares in the club's name, through the club bank account. Little did I know at the time how that interest in finance would shape my life after the disaster. I enjoyed the afternoons spent reading and used the time to study, to keep up to date with issues within the oil and gas industry, and to read my Bible and deepen my Christian faith; I was an Elder within the Apostolic Church in Middlesbrough.

I spent the afternoon of 6th July as usual. Strangely, I cannot remember in detail what I did that afternoon – in contrast to the events of the incident later that evening, which I can remember as if it happened only yesterday. However, it would have included drinking several cups of coffee, as there was always a percolator going in the production office, collecting and reading the papers and queuing for my meal at the galley before starting work. Shortly after 5.15 pm I reported for duty in the control room. My shift that night was as the Control Room Operator, as it had been the previous night, and it started as any other, with a handover from my predecessor,

Raymond Price. He brought me up to speed with the operations which were my responsibility – the oil, water-injection and produced water plants as well as the diesel pumps and the JB turbines. I was in a good mood, as it was my last shift of the week and I was going home in the morning.

Home was a large bungalow in about half an acre of land in Nunthorpe, just outside Middlesbrough, which I shared with my wife, Christine, a District Nurse, and our three children, Rachel, aged fifteen, Hannah, who was seven, and Paul, who had just turned six. I always looked forward to going home; I enjoyed the week-on-week-off lifestyle and tried to treat my week off as a week's holiday. Even though we had only moved into our bungalow two months previously, DIY and decorating were definitely not on the agenda. I had completed eighty-four hours of work during my week offshore, so my week off was 'an earned week off' which I thoroughly enjoyed. My hobbies included playing cricket, golf and squash, the children and I went to Ayresome Park, supporting Middlesbrough Football Club, and we attended church as a family. Chris and the children took the lifestyle in their stride as I had been doing it for ten years; Hannah and Paul didn't know any different. One of Chris's favourite sayings to friends and family was "I look forward to Geoff getting home, then I am usually looking forward to him going back!".

I was forty years old and, at that time, I was employed as a Production Operator by Occidental Petroleum and had been with the company in that capacity for about eight years. Except for three months which I spent on the Claymore platform in 1982, I had been on the Piper Alpha platform all that time. I didn't go into work thinking we were particularly unsafe; it was work. It was a different environment but it was an environment you soon got used to because it was similar to working onshore except the getting there and getting home, an hour-long helicopter flight to and from Aberdeen. The helicopter was usually a Sikorsky S61 and the flight was quite enjoyable in good, clear weather – which was the exception. However, the helicopters were noisy and cramped and definitely the worst part of the job in poor weather conditions. I can remember some very hairy flights. The cramped conditions added to the next worst thing, which was the smokers. If you were really unlucky, you could have one sat next to you and one or two in front and behind; the fog outside the cabin was bad enough, but the fog inside was often worse.

3

Life on an oil rig was very different. The twelve-hour shifts that we all worked took care of the bulk of the time. Add on sleeping, showering and 'messing' (oil rig language for eating) and there was only about three hours' time off to fill. I shared my cabin with a colleague called Brian Kirby, who was also a production operator, and we worked back to back shifts so, when he was on days I was on nights and vice versa, which was good as we both had the cabin to ourselves on our time off. Brian also came from the Middlesbrough area: he was a quiet lad who was interested in photography. We got on well and he was a good room-mate, other than he smoked and used to leave his full ashtray out to wind me up. However, he was equally irritated that I didn't smoke and therefore used to put his ashtray outside in the passageway each night. It became a ritual between us.

Along with the daily papers, video tapes of the previous day's TV were delivered on the first helicopter of the day. Favourites at the time included 'Match of the Day' and 'Only Fools and Horses'. These were the days before the internet, catch up TV and digital streaming. There was a recreation room where we could play table tennis and pool and films were shown in the cinema at 7.00 pm each evening, most of which weren't very good.

As events unfolded on the platform that evening, some of the men were watching the comical goings-on at an exclusive golf club in 'Caddyshack', an American sports comedy dating from 1980. As Occidental personnel, we also had our own lounge, the Oxy lounge, where we could relax, read and watch videos of the previous day's TV. Oxy staff were also allowed to phone home each evening from the production office, unlike my time on the Ninian, where we were only allowed two, five-minute phone calls a week. Generally, people did their own thing in their free time but there was a strong sense of comradeship on the rig as there were so many men living in such close quarters.

The job of Production Operator on the Piper was to look after all oil and gas process and production equipment on the platform, water injection facilities, water separation facilities, gas compression, gas condensate and electricity generating equipment, ie all of the equipment on the platform, except the drilling equipment. Each Production Operator had a designated area/equipment for which he was responsible, and he made routine checks, made sure the machinery was working properly, safely and efficiently and took readings of equipment etc. Our shift of Production Operators worked on a rota and we all worked in a different area of the platform each week, including the control room, once we were competent in that particular area.

That night there were six of us on the shift. Bob Vernon (also known as Bobby V. or 'little Bob', even though he was over 6ft tall – but 'big Bob' was even taller!) was the Lead Operator. 'Big Bob' was on holiday and the other operators on duty were Gordon Rennie, Sandy Bremner, Bob Richards (also known as 'Taxi Bob') and Erland Grieve. We had many years' experience between us and we were all competent to work in all the different areas. Erland, who was the Phase 2 Gas Plant Operator that week, hailed from the Orkney Islands and was the youngest member of the team; he'd previously worked for Occidental at the pipeline terminal on the island of Flotta. Sandy Bremner was about my age, also a family man, from the north of Scotland, who enjoyed helping on the family farm on his week off and was a good footballer. His two brothers were both professional footballers. Des had played for Aston Villa and was in the team that won the European cup in 1982 and Kevin played for Brighton. Sandy was one of the Oil and Water Operators that night, along with Gordon Rennie, who was in his mid-fifties and had extensive experience working in the Middle East and the petrochemical industry around Grangemouth. Taxi Bob, who was so named because he drove a taxi in his time off, was the Phase 1 Gas Plant Operator and had also worked in the Middle East and Grangemouth, near where he lived.

The control room on the Piper was more of a monitoring and communication room, as you couldn't actually control much from there. When I had first arrived on the Piper eight years earlier, the lack of control from the control room had been a culture shock for me compared with my previous employment at Chevron on the Ninian Southern platform and ICI on Teesside. The other function of the Control Room Operator was paperwork. All jobs have paperwork and the night shift Control Room Operator had plenty of it.

The shift started as hundreds before had done. Pre-preparing the daily production sheets, prior to completing the correct data and totals, which were the readings taken each midnight, talking, drinking coffee and then at 8:00 pm the Phase 2 Operator brought down the cakes from the galley. It got to about 9:30 pm that night and I left the control room in the hands of Little Bob and went to phone home and speak to Chris, little knowing what either of us would go through before we spoke again the following morning.

After speaking to Chris, I returned to the control room at about 9:40 pm. Nothing untoward had happened in my absence and, after chatting with Bob for a few minutes, he put his helmet on and said, "I'll have a walk round and then, whilst things are quiet, I'll go and phone home". He left me on my own and I settled down to the paperwork, prepared for a long night ahead but glad it was my last shift of the week.

About five minutes later the sequence of events started. My timescale for the disaster is thirty-five minutes, that is from the first alarm coming into the control room, up to what I call the second explosion, which was the first gigantic fireball that engulfed the platform and was the point of no return for the rig and for one hundred and sixty-seven of the two hundred and twenty-eight men who were on the Piper Alpha platform that night who lost their lives, all of them friends and colleagues of mine

2

BACK TO THE BEGINNING

My first recollection of life was starting school at Thorntree Primary school when I was five years old. Thorntree is a housing estate in East Middlesbrough on Teesside. The estate was built on farmland in the late 1940s to house people moving away from the back-to-back terraced houses of central Middlesbrough and North Ormesby. I was born in 1948 in one of those two-up-two-down terraced houses with no bathroom or hot water, the only loo being outside in the back yard. When I came along I was the fifth child and there were then seven of us living in the house and sharing the two bedrooms.

When I was two we moved to a four-bedroom council house on Thorntree estate with a bathroom, inside loo and hot and cold running water. It must have felt like sheer luxury for my mother, who worked her socks off taking care of us all. Looking back, Mam had a gruelling life. All she seemed to do was wash, clean, cook and iron and, on top of all that, she worked part-time in the local fish and chip shop.

Three more siblings followed in the next ten years, completing our family of ten. My memories of childhood are of a happy home life, spoilt only by having to attend senior school. My parents both worked hard to provide for us and home life was good. I have a lot to thank my parents for. They provided a secure and loving home and taught us all about the need to work hard and be honest; qualities that I have endeavoured to instil into my own children.

I remember an incident with Mam when she caught me out telling her a lie. Her response, which I have always remembered, was, "You will need a very, very good memory if you are going to tell lies because, if you make it up, you won't always remember what you said". It was a lesson that I learnt as a child and in later life adapted it to, "If you tell the truth you never have to remember what you said because, the next time you are asked the same question, you will give the same answer, without thinking".

My Dad worked as a foreman at the local GEC telephone factory and was definitely the boss at home. We pushed our luck with him at times, but rarely did he have to take further action. If he had to speak to us twice, that was usually enough, we took notice of him and behaved. Any trouble I encountered outside the home and particularly at school generally stayed there, as it would have been compounded by further trouble at home. I remember one occasion when I was caught playing truant from secondary school.

I disliked senior school but never managed to get time off, as I escaped all the childhood illnesses my siblings succumbed to and there was no way I could swing the lead with Mam, who knew every dodge before I even tried them. On this particular day, two of my friends from school, who were Catholics, had the day off for Ascension Day so I decided to play truant and join them and, armed with packed lunches, we all took our bikes to Redcar and had a lovely day at the seaside in the sunshine. Had it been pouring down it would still have been better than going to school. I returned home and all appeared to be going well. I even spent time pretending to do my homework and was planning a repeat the following day until disaster struck. A classmate called at our house with a note for my parents asking why I had been off school that day.

I consider myself very unlucky to have been caught, as it was the only time I ever nicked off and me and my pals had a system in place which was intended to beat the school system. At morning registration, when a pupil was marked as absent, the master would sometimes ask who lived near and send a letter to the missing pupil's parents requesting an explanation for the absence. The letters seldom reached the parents as we (the messengers) gave the letters to our pals instead of the parents and the replies to school were usually forged by John Trotter, the class forger, unless the absence was actually genuine, when the absent pupil passed the letter to his parents.

However, on this occasion, the system failed and the letter bypassed me and went straight to my parents. There was severe retribution at home, followed by double trouble at school the following day and I never dared play truant again! I was a marked absconder at school, I was closely monitored at school and at home and they had a genuine letter from my Dad to compare against any suspected forgeries. It was ironic; all the times I had taken letters home for my pals and bypassed the parents, yet I got caught first time.

One of the benefits of being part of a big family was always having somebody to play with and we played out in the street all year round. We played football in the winter and cricket in the summer, with two weeks of tennis when Wimbledon was on. Playing games was an important part of life and we were all very competitive with each other. When you won, you knew that you had won on your own, without any help and this applied to everything we did, including draughts, chess, monopoly, dominoes, cards and table tennis. You name it, we played it.

My younger brother, David, and I were sent to Sunday School at the local Church of England church and my older brother, Mike, was in the choir there. Nobody else in the family went to church except at Christmas and Easter. I wasn't impressed by this as most of my pals didn't have to go and I was sure it was simply Dad's way to get us out of the house for a few hours. When I asked him why I had to go to church when he didn't, I was told to mind my own business and do as I was told. When I moved to senior school and discovered that I was the only boy of my age who went to Sunday School I pointed this out to my Dad and, much to my surprise, he agreed that I could stop going. Hurrah! As usual, there was a sting in the tail; David and I were given the choice of attending the Sunday morning or evening service instead. Initially I was very disappointed but it turned out to be a winner, as attending church on a Sunday qualified you for going to the Church youth club on a Sunday and Monday evening. I loved the youth club and went away to camps each year with the local and town youth groups, including a particularly notable trip to Germany in 1966, a tale which I will return to in chapter three.

Money wasn't an abundant commodity at home but we were well fed and adequately clothed without being posh. Mam budgeted from Thursday (pay day) to Tuesday (family allowance day) on a week by week basis. We didn't have fancy holidays, just the odd away day to Redcar, except for one year when we all flew to Jersey for a week's holiday. Dad had won some money on the football pools. Unlike some of the children on the estate we always had new shoes when needed but I also had some hand-me-downs from my older brother, Mike, in particular things like football boots and wellingtons that he grew out of. I was glad that I went to a different school than Mike as, at least, my school uniform was always new.

My parents were both honest and hard-working and we were taught about the benefits and the necessity of hard work. The principles that nothing comes easy and you only get out of life what you put in to it were instilled in all of us from an early age. As soon as I was old enough, I got a job to supplement my pocket money, which wasn't a commodity I received much of. I suppose that when you had eight children you couldn't afford to pay much per head. We all received a penny pocket money for each year old we were from both Mam and Dad. By the age of twelve I received twelve pennies (one shilling) off my Dad and the same off Mam, a grand sum of two shillings, which is equivalent to ten new pence, per week. Even in 1960 two shillings didn't go very far, especially as smoking was compulsory if you wanted to be cool.

My first job was as a paperboy and, when I first started, I could hardly carry the bag, especially on a Sunday morning when the most papers had to be delivered. The main negative of being a paperboy with evening deliveries was always having to be there. In those days, there was always a queue of other lads after your job if you missed a shift so there was no time off. This was a real bind in the school holidays as me and my pals liked to go out for the day. We would go to the Eston Hills, Roseberry Topping, Great Ayton or Redcar, on the coast. The boating lakes in Albert Park in Middlesbrough and Locke Park in Redcar were also popular. We would pool our money, then two of us would hire a boat, rented out at a rate per person, row around the corner and everyone else would jump in. We had some seriously overloaded boats but that didn't worry us, keeping the boat out of sight of the attendant was our main objective.

Eventually I got a better job helping 'Harry' the milkman; better because I only had to work on a morning, and I did this for about three years, up to leaving school at the age of fifteen. The jobs did help but two of my little schemes were far more successful at supplementing my income. Scheme one was seasonal but very profitable and consisted of collecting and selling apples. John Trotter, my friend from school, and I used to go around the 'posh' houses and collect the windfalls. There were always a lot of windfalls once we got into the garden, as we would climb the trees and 'encourage' the apples to fall. With full haversacks, we would arrive at school the next day and quickly sell the apples to the other boys. John was an excellent business partner from my point of view because, as soon as he had enough for twenty cigarettes, he was off to the shops, dumping his apples onto me. John was a serious smoker where it was more of an image thing for me. I could do without them but he needed them.

The sale of cigarettes was my best scheme and enabled me to smoke all through senior school. It worked like this. The most popular cigarettes among the smokers were Woodbines, a strong cigarette without a filter tip, which retailed at ten for 1s 9d; filter tips were for 'cissies' at that time. At school, there was a very good market for single cigarettes and one Woodbine sold for a minimum price of 3d. Based on that minimum price, I could sell seven cigarettes for 3d each, smoke the other three and always had enough money to buy another packet of ten. (i.e. seven times 3d equals 1s 9d.) The plan usually worked like clockwork; sometimes I received a little more than 3d each if there weren't many cigarettes available, which allowed me to give or subsidise the purchase for some of the tough lads, who in turn helped keep the bullies off my back. My first lesson in economics! The biggest problem to my little enterprise was my older brother Mike, who was always cadging fags off me, which played havoc with my cash flow.

Looking back, the two blights of my life at that time were my size, or lack of it, and the time spent at school. My two older brothers were both over six feet, whilst I was consistently the smallest at senior school. To my chagrin even my younger brother, David, overtook me in height in our teens and could 'hold his own' with me in physical scraps. In his eyes, the pecking order within our family didn't apply to me because of my size. David was two years younger than me and was the best fighter in the area for his age. I remember one occasion when we were fighting and he was getting the better of me until I hit him a tremendous blow in the face, cutting his lip and breaking three front teeth. Mam was furious and sent me to get Dad, who was having his pre-Sunday lunch pint in the local pub. Dad, who then had to take David to hospital to have the bits of tooth picked out of his lip and have his face stitched, was equally furious and sent me to my bedroom for the rest of the day. Physical punishment from Dad was rare, as the worst punishment was being confined to your room. There were no TVs, computers or mobile phones in those days, just a bed to lie on and a ceiling to stare at.

My school life holds few happy memories once I left primary school. Infant school is a distant memory, a vague recollection being time spent on the naughty square. However, I do have happy memories of my time at Thorntree Junior school. I discovered that I enjoyed maths and, not only did I enjoy maths, but I was good at it. My height had not yet become an issue and, at the age of eleven, I passed the scholarship and spent the next four and a bit years at Middlesbrough Technical School. I still have an affinity for Thorntree Primary school, where I am Vice-chair of the governors and Chair of the finance committee. Thorntree estate is now a socially deprived area and I share the same passion that the other governors, the headteacher, teachers and support staff have, which is to try to give the children from the estate the best start in life that they can. I firmly believe that education and good discipline are essential, though unfortunately I didn't realise that whilst I was at school.

My years at Middlesbrough Technical School were not happy years. I was the smallest lad in the school and suffered verbal and physical bullying by the other lads, the prefects and, worst of all, the teachers. I could cope with the verbal bullying by the other lads, as I've never been short of something to say but, after I won the verbal jousting, I inevitably lost the physical. The prefects were the bane of my life. Supposedly the 'good boys' they were the worst bullies I have ever encountered. There would be physical abuse, followed by lines, followed by a report to the Headmaster for incomplete or untidy lines, which usually resulted in the cane. Acceptable levels of discipline in schools were very different in the 1950s and 1960s than they are today, and I can think of three teachers who would get prison sentences now for their actions. Potentially it could have been a very good education; in practice, it was spoiled by a few teachers who were in the wrong profession.

I left school in November 1963, aged fifteen. Most of my pals had left the previous summer and were working but my parents had encouraged me to stay on and sit my 'O' Levels. I thought I could stick another year but I was wrong and, in the November, asked my Dad if I could leave. The conversation was very short and to the point – I couldn't leave school without a job. That gave me the green light to start job-hunting and I soon secured a position as a shop assistant in the Men's shoe department with the Middlesbrough Co-operative Society. I hadn't given the type of job much thought other than, ironically, I didn't want a job where I would get dirty. It was whilst working at the Co-op that I met my wife-to-be, Christine, but that's another story.

3

TIME TO GET AN EDUCATION

School was over and it was time to get on with life and go out to work. I had been warned that I would find the real world tougher than school. It was, but, most of the time, I didn't regret leaving school. There were a few moments of regret, one of them being when my friends got their 'O' Level results, some with good results, but most of them then followed me into the world of work, with only the odd one staying on to study for 'A' Levels. Going to university was not even considered.

One friend, who shall remain nameless, sat and failed his maths 'O' Level four times and, if I ever mentioned the fact that I might have passed, would nonchalantly ask me, "By the way, how many 'O' Levels did you get?", obviously knowing that I had none. More about him later, as he provided me with a good incentive for future study.

The hours at the Co-op were longer than school and they were sticklers for timekeeping, which didn't bother me too much, but I quickly learnt that being late, even by one minute, was not advisable. I did miss the holidays and missed my Saturday afternoons at Ayresome Park watching the Boro; Saturday was now a working day.

I was paid just over four pounds per week; I gave Mam my wages and got one-pound pocket money, plus my bus fares and dinner money. My lack of height worked to my advantage now as I paid half-fare on the bus and kept the difference. I'd stopped smoking the weekend after leaving school, which saved me money and enabled me to get away with paying half-fare on the bus. Mam had said, "I know that you smoke and, now you've started work, you can smoke in the house but I can tell you it's harder to give up smoking than it is to start and, if you smoke, you'll never have any money." I took her advice to heart and stopped there and then; after all I no longer had anyone to sell them to.

I hadn't given the job much thought when I applied; it had merely been a means to leave school. However, fortunately for me, Middlesbrough Co-operative Society was a good employer, who treated their employees well and encouraged them to educate themselves with night school and day release schemes, though you had to prove your commitment to night school for a couple of years before being allowed day release.

The first evening class I enrolled for was Business Studies. I was a bit apprehensive at first but was agreeably surprised, as I didn't struggle and found that I was as good as the other students – and slightly better than some. We had a good teacher who wanted to help and actually encouraged us. After my experiences at school I found this bizarre, but good and I discovered that I enjoyed learning. I finished the course, never missing a class, and, to my surprise, passed the exam with over ninety percent, thus gaining a distinction. Book-keeping and accountancy were the next courses I attended and passed, thus qualifying for day release at the local college. I could blame circumstances and other people for my wasted years at school, whereas in reality I have to hold my hand up and take responsibility for being a bad student. However, I now worked hard at making up for the lost time at school, was enthusiastic about my studies and went on to pass human relations, shop management and staff development and training, amongst others. Looking back, I'm very grateful that I was given another chance; everybody isn't as fortunate as I was.

Two weeks after I started work a very attractive red-headed girl called Christine started working at the Co-op. I took a real fancy to her and remember asking my boss how old she was. "Seventeen and too old for you" was the answer and, at the time, I thought he was probably right. Why would an attractive seventeen-year-old girl want to go out with a fifteen-year-old lad who was shorter than her? I decided, wrongly as it turned out, that it was a non-starter.

I referred earlier to a friend who couldn't pass his maths 'O' Level. After failing it for the fourth time the usual verbal jousting started and, after much ridicule at my lack of 'O' Levels, I rose to the bait and bet him five pounds (at least two weeks' net income) that I could pass it first time as long as I could attend a refresher course at night school. He agreed and I enrolled at the local Further Education college. I was rusty and asked lots of questions in the class; I was now eighteen and had left school at fifteen. To my chagrin, two of my friend's female colleagues from work were also on the course and they found my ignorance very amusing. It was reported back to him and he gained considerable mileage over the next few weeks, as he gleefully reminded me of any questions I'd asked. Thankfully the two girls packed in half way through the course, leaving me free to ask my 'daft' questions.

Eventually exam enrolment time came and I had to pay for myself. It was one pound to register for 'O' Levels then ten shillings (equivalent of fifty pence) per subject, so one pound and fifty pence to sit the maths exam. As I was filling in the paperwork, I realised that, for another ten shillings, I could also take English Language 'O' Level. I handed over the princely sum of two pounds and sat and passed both Maths and English. I gained a great deal of satisfaction from collecting the winnings from my five-pound bet. However, we stayed good friends in our teens and twenties and still see each other occasionally.

Christine still worked at the Co-op and, at the grand age of seventeen, by which time I was just taller than her (Christine was five feet and half an inch) I plucked up the courage to ask her out. We'd been going out for about nine months when I got the chance to go to Germany with the youth club on an exchange visit to Middlesbrough's twin town, Oberhausen. I was very excited at the prospect but had to save hard to pay for the trip. There wasn't long so something had to give – and that was Chris. I told her that I couldn't afford to go out with her and save for Germany so it was 'bye, bye Christine'; she was not impressed with my decision!

When we arrived in Oberhausen we understood why it was twinned with Middlesbrough as, like the Boro, it was an industrial town with many steel and chemical works. Being an exchange visit we had an organised programme of trips, including a tour of the Crupps steel works and a trip down a coal mine at Bochum. We weren't ungrateful but, in the 1960s, we had our fill of steel works and coal mines back home. The best trip we went on was to the Mohne and Eider dams, which were breached and made famous by the 'Dam Busters' and to hear the German guide give details of what had happened was fascinating.

Outside of the official visits we had a great time. We stayed in a local youth hostel and round the back was a working men's club where we were made very welcome. We had to be back in the hostel and in bed by 10.00 pm but, as soon as we were checked in for the night, we were out of the window and round to the club. In Germany, it was legal to drink at sixteen and drinks were cheap so I thoroughly enjoyed this aspect of the local culture. All in all, it was an excellent holiday subsidised by Middlesbrough Council as a cultural trip. We certainly learnt a lot about the local culture, as did one or two of the leaders who knew what was going on with us but turned a blind eye, as we knew what they were up to.

Shortly after the trip to Germany my pals and I all turned eighteen and started spending our free time at the local pub. We'd outgrown the youth club so had no need to attend church anymore and I didn't give church or God much thought until I got married. Unfortunately I also spent less time with my younger brother, David, as he couldn't come to the pub with us.

Later that year, on Saturday 10th December 1966, I arrived home from work at about 6.00 pm to see a police car outside the house next door. Initially I didn't give it much thought, as there were often police at the house next door but, what a shock I got when I walked into our kitchen to find two coppers sat there. I immediately demanded, "Where's Mam?" to be told she'd gone upstairs to lie down. Asking the same question about Dad revealed that he was upstairs looking after her. I was bemused by this; Mam should have been cooking my tea and Dad was usually at the pub on a Saturday afternoon, having a few drinks and a bet on the horses. My first thought was that there must have been a shortage of winners for him to be home this early.

My plans for the evening were tea, wash, clean shirt and out with my pals into Middlesbrough, as we did every Saturday night. The coppers said they wanted a word with me so I sat down, still a bit distracted and wondering about my tea and what was going on. When they started talking to me they hit me with a bombshell; David had been knocked down by a car on Stockton Road on his way home from playing football for the local youth club (he was a very good footballer) and had died on the road. At eighteen years old, that was the first time that I thought the earth had stopped turning.

I couldn't help myself and started crying; David would have been sixteen the following January and had been a major part of my life since he was born. When we were younger we had been more like twins as he was big for his age and I was small; we'd laughed together, cried together, fought together and played together. One of the policemen asked me how old I was and, when I said eighteen, he suggested I stopped crying and acted like a man to support my Mam and Dad, not something that would be said nowadays. I didn't argue and took his advice, not knowing what else to do. Eventually my poor Mam and Dad came downstairs and went off with the police to identify David's body. I can't think of anything worse for a parent to have to do.

I was given the task of contacting our older siblings and started with Mike, number four in the pecking order and closest to me in age. Mike was at his girlfriend's house and I had to get the bus to her house. Nowadays we take for granted easy access to phones and cars but in 1966 only 'posh' people had one or the other and only very posh people had both; we had neither. With the help of his friends, Mike contacted our eldest three siblings whilst I stayed at home with the younger two.

My memory of the rest of the evening is blurred as all the family came around, though I do remember my pals calling for me on their way into Middlesbrough and being really upset as they all knew David. I was eighteen, at the time and I found it very tough to take as did the rest of the family.

We were a close, loving family; it hit us all hard but my parents were really, really devastated. My Dad had always taken the lead in the family but, as I look back, family dynamics changed after David's death and the power base gradually shifted to Mam, as Dad tried to do everything he could for her. Life has to go on and eventually it did in our family, although at the time you cannot imagine how it can. People say time is a great healer; I'm not sure about that – you accept it and get on with things, but the memories and sense of injustice never go away. At the time, I couldn't conceive that I would ever feel pain of that intensity again, but I was wrong.

I continued to work at the Co-op and the company started a trainee department store management scheme, which I applied for and got accepted on to. Another pay rise and further day release giving me the opportunity to attend college and gain more in-house qualifications. In 1969, a few months before my twenty-first birthday, I spotted an advert in the paper for a job at the local newspaper, the Middlesbrough Evening Gazette. The job was for a Trainee Display Advertising Representative, with a good starting salary and a company car. It stated that applicants should have five 'O' Levels and be creative; I didn't have five 'O' Levels and am not in the least bit creative but, nothing ventured, nothing gained, so I applied and, after two interviews, got the job, thus starting a new chapter in my life and career. The qualifications I'd gained through my further education studies helped me to get the job: without them I doubt I would have even got an interview.

4

BUILDING A HOME

I was offered the job of Trainee Display Advertising Representative and started the following Monday morning. The first task I was given was to find the Transport Manager and collect my car. It was a Hillman Super Minx, registration FDC 926E. The registration has stuck in my mind, as it was such a perk in Middlesbrough in 1969 to have a company car with free petrol. When I went home that night it was one of only three cars parked in the whole street and all the neighbours came out to admire it.

I worked at the Gazette for four years and loved the job; it was unbelievable for me as an impressionable twenty-year-old. I was very well mentored, both professionally and socially, and grew up quickly. The Middlesbrough Evening Gazette had a great reputation in the 1960s and 1970s and our business cards would get us into all the local clubs and sporting events. Looking back, I feel as if I would have had to pinch myself to realise that I wasn't dreaming.

There was a good deal of freedom for the reps but it was a very target driven job. As long as you hit your monthly target and the team hit the department's target, Mitch Hatfield (the boss) and his supervising underlings left you alone. However, when a particular promotion was falling behind, then the muck would hit the fan and we would all have to work extra hard to make a success of it and make sure the department hit its target.

The very first week I was there Mitch asked if I was a Boro fan; when I replied positively, he asked if I would like to go to Blackburn the following evening to watch the match. Naively I replied that I didn't finish work till 5.00 pm so wouldn't get there in time. We finished at about four o'clock and four of us set off with Mitch in his company car to Ewood Park. Sadly, we lost the match but that is something you get used to when you support the Boro!

Another fond memory is from cup final day on 26th April 1969; this was the first time I saw live colour television. Mitch invited the team, about sixteen of us, to his house at Marske-by-the-Sea, to watch the match. We met in the Middle House pub at lunchtime then continued the drinking at his home. When I saw the green grass of Wembley, the black and red shirts of Manchester City and the blue shirts of Leicester City I was gob-smacked; the quality of the colour was amazing. I remember the occasion well; Neil Young scored for Man City and Allan Clark of Leicester was man of the match. I'm sure it's stuck in my memory because it seemed such a miracle at the time, though nowadays is something we take for granted. Three years earlier, in 1966, I'd watched England win the World Cup and the pitch was grey, Germany's shirts were white and England's grey. We used to watch snooker in black and white and the only two balls which were distinguishable were the black ball and the white ball, all the others were different shades of grey, leading to the famous comment, 'the pink ball is the ball behind the yellow ball', both balls appearing an identical shade of grey to the viewers.

Two years after I started work at the Evening Gazette I married Christine Balding, who I'd met seven years earlier at the Co-op; after an on-off courtship and, despite my decision to go to Germany a few years earlier, we finally made it to the altar. She was an attractive, red-haired girl who was very placid most of the time but, like most of us, had her moments of temper. They made strong engagement rings in the 1960s and I remember hers bouncing off the cobbles on several occasions when I took her home after a night out. We would usually fall out about our next meeting, or lack of it, as she didn't understand the importance of football or cricket, especially when they fell on her next day off. My poor attitude combined with her quick temper resulted in the ring coming off yet again. Somehow it remained intact, despite the rough treatment it was given, as has our marriage; we're still together nearly fifty years later.

We were married on 19th September 1970. It was a very low-key wedding by today's standards. Chris's Dad was a very generous Irishman who gave away anything he had as soon as he got it; if and when he had money, he spent it. Money wasn't a large commodity in my family, so we both knew that, whatever wedding we had, we would have to pay for it ourselves. As you may have gathered by now, I've always been fiscally minded and my first priority was to save enough for a deposit for our own home. I had watched my parents pay rent all my life and yet not own a brick of their own home. We found a new-build, two-bedroomed bungalow for the princely sum of three thousand pounds, with an additional three hundred for central heating – living in the 'frozen north' it was well worth it. Our other extravagance was a colour television, which was a real novelty at the time, as none of my friends or family had ever seen a colour television, never mind owned one. Everyone, and I mean everyone, who came to our house went away as impressed as I'd been when I watched the football match at Mitch's house. My older brother, Alan, and my dad thought the horse racing was particularly amazing. Looking back, I missed an opportunity as the colour TV market exploded.

We were married at the local Methodist church, a compromise as I didn't go to church and had very little faith and Christine was an enthusiastic church-goer who attended the Apostolic Church[2] in Middlesbrough. I found her beliefs a bit strange; she went to church at least twice on a Sunday, church midweek and sometimes church on a Saturday. She didn't drink or smoke or gamble. It sounded a pretty miserable life to me but she wasn't miserable, she was really good fun, and the people I met who went to her church all seemed happy, which I found quite amazing. She was certainly cheap to take out, which helped our saving.

A couple of times I'd given in and attended church with her. I was amazed, they were playing musical instruments, including the obligatory tambourine, clapping their hands, shouting 'halleluiah' and singing with great enthusiasm and gusto – very different to my childhood experiences of church. I was prepared to get married in her church, which didn't look at all like a church, down a back street in Middlesbrough, but her Vicar (who they called a Pastor) wouldn't marry us. He couldn't condone Christine

---

2   The Apostolic Church is a Christian Pentecostal denomination.

marrying an unbeliever, which I was at that time. It didn't bother me but Chris was upset with him; later I became very good friends with that Pastor.

I was employed at the Gazette for four years and enjoyed my time working there. Towards the end of the four years Mitch left the Gazette and the new boss came from one of the company's newspapers at Slough or Reading, somewhere 'down south'. He was totally alien to the North East and thought Middlesbrough was the 'back of beyond'. Our culture as Middlesbrough football supporters was discouraged, as he thought that football was a game for hooligans and barbarians. That didn't go down well with us but we had to adjust. I no longer enjoyed the job and me and him didn't get on, so I started looking for a new job and got a good position as Advertising and Sales Promotion Manager at a large carpet retailer in Redcar, one of our major advertisers.

After leaving the Co-op, Chris had trained and qualified as a nurse; she worked at Middlesbrough General Hospital for three years and then got a job as a District Nurse, making her calls on a bike, which she borrowed from my sister Anne for the first few months, as she hadn't yet passed her driving test. She quickly passed her test and bought her first car, a white Mini which she bought off the Middlesbrough footballer, Frank Spraggon. With two wages coming in we continued to improve our home. We moved to another bungalow on a new development south of Middlesbrough, the first of eight house moves during our married life, all within a few miles' radius. I've lived and worked in Middlesbrough all my life, except for my time offshore, and have often been asked why I want to live in that dump.

I can understand why the general perception of Middlesbrough is that it's a dump; when people visit the area for work they see the chemical and steel works, visiting football supporters arriving at the Riverside Stadium see a chemical works and run-down docks and the train through Middlesbrough travels through old, run-down industrial areas. Any news items shown on television regarding Middlesbrough tend to portray back-to-back terraced houses and a skyline shot of the Transporter Bridge with the chemical works north of the river in the background.

However, there is another side to Middlesbrough; it was formed as a 'new town' in the 1830s on the banks of the River Tees and has spread southwards towards North Yorkshire (it was originally in North Yorkshire) providing some very desirable places to live and visit. The countryside and coastline are magnificent, the Victorian seaside town of Saltburn, picturesque Whitby and the North Yorkshire Moors and National Parks all being within easy reach. Being a 'Smoggie' as the Sunderland fans call us has a lot of positives, including getting a lot of house for your money and being able to drive in relatively light traffic.

However, this isn't a travel guide to the North East, so back to family life. Our first child, Rachel Jane, was born whilst I worked at the carpet firm in Redcar, on Christmas Day in 1972. We were chuffed to bits by Rachel's arrival and sixteen months later our first son, Daniel Geoffrey, was born at Eastertime. Chris continued to work after Rachel was born but, after Daniel's birth in April 1974, she gave up work to look after the children and we lived on my wage from the carpet retailers.

I enjoyed the job at the carpet firm and learnt a lot whilst I was there. I made it my mission to understand and get involved in every aspect of the business, from carpet fitting to sales and accounts. I made improvements in the profits of the business and rearranged some of the practices in all the departments, unfortunately also making a few enemies along the way, which resulted in me being 'shown the door' when I agreed to replace an expensive carpet for a customer to settle a complaint that was getting nasty. One of the bosses was on holiday at the time and had a very different view of the situation to me when he returned. We had a strong disagreement about it and he settled the disagreement by giving me one week's wages in lieu of notice. It isn't very often that I am speechless, but I was that day. One week's wages were not going to go far, with a mortgage to pay and two young children and a wife to support.

I got another job at a carpet shop in Stockton as a stop gap and quickly started making plans to move on. It's sometimes strange how things work out; in my drive to improve efficiency at the Redcar firm I had found that I had an aptitude for fitting carpets. When investigating complaints from customers, the complaint would often be genuine but relatively small and, after seeing it, reporting it and sending out a fitting team to rectify it, I realised that I was better off attending to it there and then if I could, saving a considerable amount of time and money. I started carrying a set of tools with me.

I resigned from the job in Stockton after a couple of months and started working for myself, selling and fitting carpets. Using contacts I'd made in the carpet industry, I registered a company name, opened accounts with two major wholesalers, opened a bank account and, for the first time in my life, took out a bank loan to buy a vehicle. I bought a Volkswagen twelve-seater, long enough to take a twelve-foot roll of carpet without bending it and with the added advantage of being used as a taxi for football matches, race meetings and nights out; getting paid to go and watch sport was excellent.

Business was up and down but profitable and I enjoyed being self-employed; it was a steep learning curve. However, I encountered a few hiccups, including one that nearly bankrupted me. I secured the contract to carpet a new night club in the town. At first all went well, the job was completed on time and the club opened but the bill wasn't paid, causing me severe cash flow problems – no materials until I could pay my suppliers, no sales, no work and no money to live off. Eventually, as I neared desperation point, the bank extended my overdraft, insisting on a second charge against our home, which neither Chris nor I were happy about. Eventually I was paid but it was a situation I never wanted to return to.

Business was good for a few years but suffered from a decline in the hot summer of 1975; business picked up again at Christmas but there was a repeat during the hot summer of 1976. Along with the rain drying up, so did business. It was great weather for cricket and I had plenty of time to play it, as there was very little work about, but things were getting desperate again. As the days went by the answer to the problem became more and more obvious, however much I tried to postpone it. I needed to get a job. One of the lads I played cricket with, an old school friend called John Meek, worked at ICI and told me they were recruiting process operators, as ICI was expanding on Teesside. The jobs were for shift workers and full training would be given. There was nothing to lose by applying and working shifts would fit around my business. John got me an application form and, after mandatory IQ tests, two interviews and a medical, I had a new job – not one that matched my initial work requirement of not getting my hands dirty, which was the only thought I had about a career when I left school.

5

THE NORTH SEA BECKONS

It was a big cultural change for me at twenty-eight years old; I had never got my hands dirty, never mind working in industry, never had to join a union, never had to clock-on and clock-off and never worked shifts before. The job was a financial necessity and I thought I'd just have to make the best of it but it turned out to be a pleasant surprise and a very interesting job. My colleagues were helpful and I had a lot of respect for the supervisors and control room operators who knew their jobs and the complicated process and control equipment very well.

All credit to ICI who did things properly. The first four weeks were on a programmed, classroom-based induction course, including plant tours and assessment tests. At the end of the course we were allocated jobs on different plants; I was given a process operator's job on the Olefines 5 plant. I was kitted out and reported for work on my first shift. There was a big shift team of approximately twenty operators, three area foremen and a shift supervisor. I was given a grand tour, then spent four months shadowing a more experienced operator until one shift, without warning, the supervisor said, "Put your helmet on, we're going for a walk." After a walk round the plant and in depth questioning about its workings, I was put on the shift rota as a qualified operator for an area of the plant.

I had worked for ICI for about five months when my father died at the age of sixty-two. I had been working the night shift and, as I arrived home at about 6.00 am, I noticed the kitchen light was on and Rachel and Daniel were up and having breakfast. Chris had received a phone call to say that my Dad had been taken to Middlesbrough General Hospital with a heart attack, so I went straight to the hospital. Mam and all my siblings were already there but nothing could be done and he died later that day, surrounded by his family. It was another very sad time for our family. We were a close family and my Dad's death affected all of us; you only get one Dad and now he was gone. He had been a good man who worked hard all his adult life to provide for us and had been a good role model.

My parents' home had always been the main meeting place and focal point for family gatherings, but this changed and my older sister Hazel's home increasingly became the focal point to take some of the pressure off Mam. Mam had to vacate her home after Dad died; years earlier he had been made redundant from the GEC after working there for over twenty years. He didn't get any redundancy pay and had got a job as a school caretaker and their house came with the job. Although Redcar and Cleveland Council had a responsibility to rehouse Mam in or near the school house, she ended up accepting a house in a different and inferior area once the new caretaker was appointed because she felt she was living in his and his family's house, going against the advice of all her children. It was a difficult move for her.

Rachel had just turned four and Daniel was approaching his third birthday; they both loved going to Grandma and Grandad's house, where they were completely spoiled. At first they asked where Grandad was and my memory is that we told them that he was with the Angels in Heaven. I didn't go to church at the time but found it a comforting thought and definitely better than the thought that he had gone to hell, or had just disappeared into nothingness. Rachel and Daniel quickly accepted what had happened and the sweetie cupboard remained high on their list of priorities at both Grandma's and Auntie Hazel's houses.

I'd only been at ICI for five months when Dad died so didn't qualify for a day off for his funeral, in contrast to the Evening Gazette where I had time off to go to a football match in my first week. ICI told me that 'rules are rules'; however, I was allowed to put in a day's holiday so that I could attend.

Apart from that things were going well at work; I was learning the job and most of the men I worked with were experienced and very helpful. I was also doing some carpet work between shifts so our finances were improving fast. ICI was building a new plant, Olefines 6, at Wilton, near Redcar, and jobs were being advertised internally; their plan was that the employees for the new plant would start work during completion and train on the job. This appealed to me as I wanted to learn as much as I could about my new job. I had wasted my opportunities at school and had learnt a valuable lesson which has stood me in good stead in subsequent years.

I successfully applied for a transfer to the new plant, resulting in a pay rise and a six-month period of day shifts whilst the plant was completed. However, things didn't go to plan due to strikes and 'go-slows' from the construction crews building the plant and the six-month training period extended to nearly eighteen months. It was excellent, it was like an eighteen-month apprenticeship on full wages and full shift allowance, better than I could have hoped for and I learnt a lot about chemical processes and plant operations and systems during this time.

It was now 1978 and ICI were losing a lot of experienced operators and supervisors to tax-free jobs in Saudi Arabia, Iran (pre-revolution), Iraq, Lybia and Algeria. The offshore oil fields in the North Sea were also recruiting and looking for experienced staff to operate the platforms as the construction phases neared completion.

The Olefines 6 plant was nearly completed and getting ready for start-up and all the shift staff were put back onto their shift pattern. One day, between my shifts, I was working on a carpet job for one of my brother's neighbours, Dave Gutteridge. I had known Dave for a few years; he was an ex-ICI process operator who now worked offshore for British Petroleum in the Forties field. He told me that an ICI mate of his, John Chapman, had gone to work for Chevron and that they were recruiting for their platforms in the Ninian field. He phoned John and John got me an application form for Chevron. I applied and was very quickly invited to Aberdeen for an interview for a production operator's job on the Ninian Southern platform.

It was a bizarre interview, which I travelled to Aberdeen for; it lasted about five minutes. I was interviewed by Z. Z. Rushing, the Platform and Production Manager for the Central platform. I went into his office and sat down facing him across his desk with my application form in front of him. "Well Geo, Goff, Gee, Geof, Geef" he started, at which point I politely interrupted him and said, "Geoffrey". "Well, there you are, I've got a funny name as well, that's why people call me Zee Zee. I see that you work as an operator at ICI and you come from Middlesbrough." After establishing where Middlesbrough was (he was American) and what the travel links were like, he said, "Thanks for coming to Aberdeen today, let me sort out your expenses." I gave him my flight ticket and taxi receipts and he came back with the cash there and then. It was a total contrast to the rigorous recruitment procedures at ICI and I went home bemused at what had happened. The following week I got a letter offering me a job with Chevron and I resigned from ICI. I did very well out of ICI but, as a company, they got a very poor return for their investment in me.

I started working for Chevron in October 1978, reporting for work at the Chevron training centre in Golden Square, Aberdeen. The address proved to be very appropriate as the expenses we were paid during our training were very generous. There were about thirty of us who were going to work offshore, a mix of trades including operators, electricians, mechanical fitters and tiffies (instrument articifers) on a week's induction course.

We were welcomed to the company and introduced to the Chevron expense claim form, a G0165, and the advance expense claim form and told to ask for expenses of two hundred pounds. Two days later we left with cheques for two hundred pounds, repeated again on the Thursday for those of us who were travelling from Newcastle and Teesside. The Chevron Office was in a building called Caledonian House on Union St in Aberdeen and we quickly coined the phrase, "Pass Caledonian House and collect two hundred pounds". When we cashed our cheques you usually got Scottish Bank notes, which looked a bit like Monopoly money. It definitely wasn't Monopoly money and, in this first week, I had gone from earning less than one hundred pounds a week to being given four hundred pounds expenses tax-free and a pay rise. I thought I was dreaming.

The training plan was four weeks onshore, doing survival, fire-fighting and basic laboratory testing courses, which was then followed by four weeks of 'fill-in' courses. The first four weeks were really interesting and we lived the high life, flying up and down to Aberdeen, staying in four-star hotels with swimming pools and squash courts, nice food and wine (more like a few beers!) and taxis everywhere. All we had to do was collect the receipts, fill in the G0165, pass Caledonia House and keep collecting two hundred pounds. The second four-week block wasn't as interesting from a course point of view; there were basic process modular courses, which felt like being back at elementary school after the high-quality process training I'd received at ICI.

We all started to get a bit fed up, as the 'training' lasted for twelve weeks, but Chevron were paying us and couldn't send us offshore until the production plant and equipment were ready. We would have occupied beds which were needed for people who had work to do on the rig; beds on the rig were at a premium and there was no work for production operators yet. I felt a bit guilty living the high life in Aberdeen while Chris was back home juggling work and looking after two young children. Chris had gone back to work as a school nurse at Netherfields Primary School in 1977, as the hours fitted around the children; Rachel was five years old and Daniel four and they went to nursery during the school day.

At Chevron we were allocated into two crews, blue and red, to cover the shift pattern of two weeks on and two weeks off; one crew was at home, the other on the platform doing twelve-hour shifts covering nights and days, the crew change being every other Tuesday. I was allocated to the blue crew and, when we worked the rotas out, the blue crew was due to be working offshore on Christmas Day in 1978.

However bored I was with the time filling courses, I was desperately hoping they would continue over Christmas and New Year. As part of a big family, Christmas was a special time for us and we all came together; it would also be Rachel's sixth birthday and I wanted to spend the time with her, Daniel and Chris. I was hopeful right up until Saturday 8th December when the dreaded telegram arrived, telling me to report to Dyce airport in Aberdeen on Tuesday 11th December and bring my offshore clothing and equipment. My first trip offshore and my first Christmas away from my family. Although fourteen days later was Christmas Day, the crew change would not be until the 27th December as there weren't any flights on Christmas Day or Boxing Day, so my first trip extended to sixteen days, including working over Christmas. I wished I'd been allocated to the red crew who were going to spend Christmas at home.

Monday morning dawned and I was flying to Aberdeen in the afternoon to stay overnight and check in at Dyce airport at 8.00 am the following day. I had breakfast with Rachel and Daniel before they left for school and nursery with Chris. Thirty-nine years later I can still see them both in the backseat of her maroon Mini, as if it were yesterday, Daniel standing on the seat waving to me. Little did I know it would be the last time I would ever see him.

The big day finally arrived; having spent twelve weeks in Aberdeen and Montrose and spending loads of Chevron's money, it was time to go offshore and start earning my keep. The flight plan was a fixed wing plane to Sumburgh airport where we changed and flew out to the Ninian Southern platform by helicopter. The Ninian oil field is situated in the North Sea around one hundred and forty-four kilometres east-northeast of the Shetland Islands. The plane we boarded at Dyce was a small plane that carried about twenty men. It was low to the ground and had access doors like car doors at alternate sides of the plane; you simply climbed in and the door was shut behind you.

I've never been a big fan of flying, as your life is in the hands of the pilot, the maintenance crew and God; this first flight did nothing to assuage my fears. After about twenty minutes there was a British Rail quality announcement which, fortunately, we couldn't hear and half an hour later we landed at Kirkwall airport on the Orkney Islands. One of the maintenance crew came out and asked the pilot why he had landed. He replied, "The port engine packed in twenty minutes after take-off and I made it here to get it looked at." We disembarked and had a sandwich and a cuppa whilst the plane was attended to and then set off again to Sumburgh. My first helicopter flight was a bit of an anti-climax after the hairy plane journey.

Before boarding the helicopter, we had to put on our survival suits and life jackets. The survival suits were big all-in-one plastic bags with inclusive arms, legs, feet and hoods, which zipped up the front. The temperature in the North Sea is seven to eight degrees, summer and winter, and the suits were designed to retain body heat and keep you alive for longer if the helicopter had to ditch into the sea. At our survival training course, we were told we would only survive for about thirty minutes in the sea without a suit; longer with one but no one told us how much longer and thankfully I never had to find out. We didn't think the plastic bags would be much use, so we nick-named them 'body bags'.

Arriving at the Ninian Southern platform for the first time was very exciting. We had been in the helicopter for about an hour when someone spotted the platform on the horizon and we were all out of our seats and scrabbling to get a first glimpse of our new workplace, to be quickly told by the pilot to get back in our seats. My initial reactions were surprise and admiration; I was amazed at the sheer size of the rig. It was a clear day and the platform was massive on the horizon, standing some three hundred feet above sea level, with the production, accommodation and drilling derrick all stacked on top of each other; you couldn't help but marvel at the skill of those who had designed and built it and floated it out there – a big credit to British engineering.

Floating either side and next to the platform were two huge semi-submersible accommodation barges, the Borgland Dolphin and the Viking Piper. They half floated above the water line providing hotel facilities for the hundreds of contractors who were still finishing off construction. The contractors lived in what we called 'tin town', which was comprised of lots of containers with beds in them; it was rough and very basic living. The contractors were nicknamed 'bears' and they were rough and tough men.

We checked in and were given a very short induction and told to report to the control room. My first impressions were good; I shared a two-man cabin with an adjoining bathroom and the quality, quantity and choice of food in the galley was amazing; I was very glad I wasn't sleeping in 'tin town'. On reporting to the control room I met John Chapman, who had got me my original application form. He'd been working offshore for about six months and we hit it off immediately; he was ex-ICI, lived in Stockton-on-Tees and was a fellow Boro supporter. I stuck with him for my first few shifts and he showed me round whilst I got my bearings and got my overalls dirty – it didn't do to look like the new lad for long!

I soon settled into the routine; it was very similar to my previous job at ICI except the shifts were longer and you didn't go home when you clocked off. Whilst offshore Chevron only allowed us two five-minute phone calls a week which, looking back, was particularly stingy from a company that was so generous in lots of other ways. The telephone booking sheets went up each morning and there was always a scramble to put your name down, as most of us wanted a time when our children were up and around. Those calls were precious and eagerly anticipated by all of us. Then we got a bit of good news; on Christmas Day we were going to be allowed an extra ten-minute call home. This cheered me up a bit; during the training I'd been looking forward to going offshore but once I knew I'd be away for Christmas and miss Rachel's sixth birthday, a bit of a black cloud had hung over me and I'd felt despondent at the thought of being so far from my family.

6

TRAGEDY AND BELIEF

Christmas Day dawned and Chevron did us proud; all the goodies that we would have had at home were available on the platform, except for the alcohol. We worked our shift pattern but didn't actually do any work, as we weren't producing any oil and we were allowed to take things easy. We played board games and had quizzes amongst ourselves in the control room to make the best we could of the situation; after all we were there voluntarily, we were being paid to be there and it was our choice to work for Chevron.

My extra phone call was booked for five o'clock and I was really looking forward to speaking to Chris and the children. A phone box had been constructed on the platform for us to make our five-minute calls home and the calls were connected via an operator in Aberdeen who checked who you were and the number you wanted to call and then made the connection. Our phone time was very precious and it was frustrating when any of that time was lost due to connection problems. However, this extra call was to be made from one of the offices on the STD direct dial line.

I dialled my sister Hazel's home phone number, as it was our family tradition, after my dad had died, that everyone congregated at Hazel's on Christmas Day afternoon and evening. I was told that Christine and the children weren't there, as Daniel wasn't very well. Not feeling particularly alarmed at this point, I hung up and redialled our home number. The call had just connected when 'Fat Ken', the Chevron radio operator and a definite 'jobsworth', came into the room and said that I couldn't make two calls. I quickly told him that I'd dialled the wrong number, which wasn't a million miles from the truth, as I wanted to speak to my wife and she wasn't there. The phone was answered by Alan, my brother, who said the doctor was with Daniel and they were waiting for an ambulance to take him to hospital. I was picking up very concerning, negative vibes by this point and asked all the questions that you would ask as a concerned parent, but he couldn't answer any of my questions except to say that Daniel was ill.

My ten minutes were quickly up and Fat Ken terminated the call, as there were other people waiting to speak to their families. I staggered out of the office in a daze and went straight into Alan Higgin's office and told him that my young son was being rushed to hospital. Alan was the Offshore Installation Manager, the big boss, and he immediately started making phone calls to try to get me off the platform the next day.

I rang home again thirty minutes later and whoever answered the phone couldn't speak. Alan took the phone; he was so upset that he could hardly speak either but eventually managed to tell me that Daniel had died in his bed, with the doctor there, waiting for the ambulance. When David had been killed twelve years earlier and my Dad the year before, I had thought I would never feel pain of that intensity again. I was wrong. Only people who have lost a young child will be able to understand how I felt in that moment. I had a million questions that I wanted to ask between my tears but didn't get many answers between the tears at the other end. I spoke to Chris but we could hardly manage to have a conversation between our tears and there wasn't anything she could tell me, except that he started feeling poorly and went to bed showing flu-like symptoms.

In the afternoon of Christmas Day, Daniel had started to feel unwell but still wanted to go to Auntie Hazel's. He had a temperature so Chris put him to bed, much to his and Rachel's disappointment. His condition deteriorated and, even though you didn't call the doctor out in those days, especially on Christmas Day, Chris had phoned. When the doctor arrived he immediately rang for an ambulance but, by the time the ambulance arrived, my darling little boy had died. He had contracted viral pneumonia and went from feeling unwell to dying in a matter of a few hours; the final stages were very quick and the doctor did everything he could for Daniel.

If I'd been in a daze after the bad news on my first call home, I was completely gone now. I staggered back into Alan's office and all I could say was, "He's dead, he's dead". Looking back, it all feels a bit of a blur, but I do know that he tannoyed for the medic and I ended up in the sick bay where the medic 'suggested' that I lie down and he gave me some medication. Apparently, he stayed with me all night and I woke the next morning feeling hung over, struggling to process the events of the last twenty-four hours. I have no recollection of whether I phoned home again that night or even the next morning, and neither has Chris, but I suppose that I did.

Alan Higgins had told me that he would do everything in his power to get me home on Boxing Day and he did. He arranged for me to go ashore on the Bolckow helicopter, a small four-seater craft that was used for short flights between the platforms in the Ninian field, weather permitting. A car would then take me to Dyce airport in Aberdeen where a flight had been arranged with Air Ecosse to take me to Teesside airport. Air Ecosse was a Scottish commuter airline based in Aberdeen which operated in the late 1970s to mid-1980s.

The Bolckow, which had taken off from the Central platform, arrived at about eight o'clock on Boxing Day morning with two passengers already on board who had cadged a lift when they heard about my medevac flight. It was over one hundred miles to the mainland and it was squashed and very noisy in the little helicopter, but I was in no mood for talking. The pilot explained that he could only make the flight as we had a tailwind which was favourable and we would hopefully have enough fuel to reach the Scottish mainland, but nowhere near as south as Aberdeen. I wasn't interested in the wind direction or fuel shortages, I was just desperate to get off the oil rig and go home to my family.

The flight was uneventful and we landed somewhere north of Inverness in the north-east of Scotland, about one hundred and twenty miles north of Aberdeen, where I was met by a chauffeur driven car for the journey to Dyce. When I arrived at the Air Ecosse check-in desk at Dyce airport they were waiting for me, as mine was their only flight on Boxing Day, but I had to wait until noon to take off, as Teesside airport wasn't open until one o'clock. Teesside, an international airport, was shut in the morning because it was a bank holiday.

The pilot was the Air Ecosse on-call pilot over the Christmas holiday period who had been called into Gatwick airport to fly to Aberdeen, take his passenger to Teesside, then return to Gatwick. I was the only passenger on the plane and was invited to sit next to him in the co-pilot's seat. Understandably, I wasn't in the best of moods but, under the circumstances, I enjoyed the flight and found the pilot's information and instruction interesting.

As we approached Teesside at about ten minutes to one he radioed for permission to land but couldn't raise anybody and got more and more frustrated as he circled over County Durham, running low on fuel. When he finally made contact with air traffic control at ten minutes past one, ten minutes after they should have been open and ready to receive flights, he asked for permission to land and was told that he couldn't land as the airport's fire brigade were late for work. However frustrated we both were (the pilot's last words to Teesside Airport were that he was going to report them to the Civil Aviation Authority), there was nothing we could do. The flight was diverted to Newcastle airport and my lift was sent up to Newcastle to meet me, adding an additional two hours to my journey home to my family. Putting this into context with all the help and support everyone else had proffered, I felt that Teesside Airport was completely useless – and to compound my frustration I was not even offered an apology. Since that day I've always thought of Teesside Airport as a 'Mickey Mouse' airport!

I arrived home to a disaster zone. It is very hard to describe. I was relieved to get home and be with Christine and Rachel; Mam was there and most of my brothers and sisters, but the person I wanted most to be there wasn't. There were lots and lots of tears and poor Rachel was very, very upset. I don't know how much six-year-olds grasp about death, but she seemed to understand that Daniel had left the house and she wouldn't see him again. It was difficult for me to take in and the questions that I have asked for nearly forty years are: "Why?","Why did our lovely little boy have to die?", "Why did he die so quickly without any real signs of being seriously ill?", "Why couldn't the Doctor and the ambulance men save him, with all the modern medicines available?", "Why, Why, Why?". I don't know the answers, but I knew that I wasn't very pleased with this God that Christine believed in.

It was a desolate time for us all and we were all devastated, and I mean devastated. I know the correct meaning of the word and it has been one of my pet hates ever since, to hear people misuse the word, e.g. football players, team managers, match commentators, etc who talk about a player being 'devastated' because they have, for example, missed an open goal, let a goal in, missed a penalty or something equally trivial. Things that devastate you change your life. Daniel dying changed my life and a lot of other people's lives.

The day after I arrived home I made a decision which I have since regretted. After David was killed I went to the funeral parlour to see him for the last time. When I saw him in his coffin, I couldn't believe it was him, it looked nothing like him, though not because of any facial injuries. I questioned his identity and had to be assured it was David. I was upset before seeing him but even more upset afterwards. I decided then that I wouldn't do that again, as I wanted to remember people when they were alive, not as you see them in their coffins. I didn't go to see Daniel in the funeral parlour, as I wanted to remember him as the happy little boy that I loved, standing in the back of Chris's car waving to me on the day I went offshore. I've always felt that was a wrong decision and I still reproach myself about it, forty years later. Some decisions you don't get the chance to rectify.

The funeral was a very bleak day in all respects. It was really cold and it snowed as we stood in the cemetery watching his little coffin being lowered into the ground. After the funeral the bleak cloud remained, but life had to go on; we had a six-year old daughter and we needed to support each other.

I was due to go back offshore on 9th January but was told by Chevron to miss the trip and see how I felt in February. Chris also had some time off work but we both felt that sitting around, moping, feeling sorry for ourselves and doing nothing wasn't working; we both needed something to occupy our minds. Chris went back to work at the school but it was at least another six weeks before I was due to go back offshore. The big question was whether I went back to the platform or got a job at home; it was a question we asked ourselves and one that was asked by family and friends. My feeling was that I wanted to go back and give it the six-month trial period we'd originally set. Chris agreed and we decided to assess things on a trip-by-trip basis. I went offshore again on Tuesday 6th February 1979.

People at home had been very supportive, as were Chevron management, who were excellent, and my colleagues on the rig, and I really appreciated everyone's kindness. The Pastor from Chris's church was a frequent visitor, but he didn't half get on my nerves and I soon started avoiding his visits, as I came very close to losing it with him and telling him what I thought about his Jesus and his God who had taken our little boy away. I didn't care about upsetting him from my point of view but, if I had, it would have upset Chris so I decided avoidance and biting my blunt Yorkshire tongue was the best policy.

Part of me was relieved to go back offshore; I enjoyed the busyness and learning the new job. Some of my family questioned my decision and I was accused of being insensitive and selfish; I questioned it myself and found it a particular wrench leaving Rachel. Whilst on the rig I had very mixed emotions; it was exciting as the equipment was being handed over to us and we were going to produce 'first oil' (that is, export oil to the refinery). However, I couldn't get Daniel out of my head, I worried about Christine and Rachel back home and I counted the days until I could return to Middlesbrough. Much as I enjoyed my new job, I was prepared to pack it in if that was necessary. People can have their own opinions about whether I should have gone back offshore but it was a joint decision made by Chris and I.

I first met Christine in 1963 and all the time that I'd know her she'd gone to church regularly and her Christian faith was important to her. She usually went to church on a Thursday evening but on my first Thursday back home she decided to give it a miss. I didn't give it much thought until the same thing happened on the Sunday, both morning and evening. I thought it unusual but left it there until the same thing happened the following week and, when I asked her why, she said spending the time together was more important.

The two weeks at home flew by in comparison to the two weeks spent offshore and it was soon time for me to return. We decided that I should make the trip and see how she felt next time I was home so I went back offshore, back to just two five-minute phone calls a week. On returning home after my next shift cycle, it was a repeat of the previous six weeks. Chris still didn't want to go to church; she felt as though God had let her down in allowing Daniel to die. I didn't share her faith or depth of belief but could understand how she must have felt. I wasn't happy with something that I only faintly believed in and Chris was obviously struggling to cope with her faith.

Our friends and family were very supportive but, selfishly, I wanted Chris to have the support that her church and friends there gave her. My thinking was that, the more she settled back into her routine, the easier it would be for me to continue working offshore. To this end I encouraged her to go to church and offered to go with her. It wasn't much of a hardship as the cricket season hadn't started. The three of us went the following Sunday evening. I found it all a bit over-the-top, the enthusiastic singing and preacher who got very excited; it was as far removed from my youthful church attendance as chalk is from cheese.

As we sat in the church I was on my best behaviour for Chris's sake. Rachel, who was used to going to church, sat reading her books and colouring, paying no attention to what was going on. I clock-watched all the way through; after what seemed like an eternity, the service finally finished and I set my sights on a quick cuppa and a sharp exit. However, the Pastor paused and said that he believed that God was speaking to someone so they would continue the service. My heart sank and, in normal circumstances, I would have left there and then, but these weren't normal circumstances so I stayed, still on my best behaviour. The rest of the congregation continued singing and praying and Rachel continued colouring and not paying any attention to what was going on.

Completely out of the blue, Rachel pulled on my jacket and said, "Dad, it's you that God is speaking to." I was flabbergasted! If anybody else in that church, including Chris, had said that to me I would have dismissed them out of hand, but Rachel was only six and didn't really understand what she was saying or what was happening.

At that moment the biggest cynic in the room became a believer; I decided that God was speaking to me and I went to the front of church and spoke to the Pastor. I didn't see any flashing lights or feel any great emotion, I simply made a conscious decision in that moment that God was real. Different people and churches have different expressions for the decision I'd made, being born again, accepting Jesus into your life, being converted, becoming a believer. Whatever you may call it, that is what happened to me and thirty-eight years later it's a decision I've never regretted. I remember telling my Mam shortly afterwards and she said it was a phase due to our circumstances and it would soon pass – but it hasn't.

I now believed in God and Jesus Christ, his Son and my Saviour. At last I was on the same wavelength – or 'singing from the same hymn sheet' – as my wife, this attractive girl that I'd met fifteen years earlier with the weird beliefs about God. Chris was thrilled with my decision, it helped her to get back on track with her own faith and brought us closer together. We started to go to church together and she was a big help to me in answering questions about my new-found faith. My biggest stumbling block in the early days was constantly asking God why Daniel had to die, a question neither of us could answer. Now and then I still ask Him, but I'm not expecting an answer this side of heaven.

My life changed. Some of it straightaway and some more subtly without me noticing or trying, as my values and attitudes to life and other people changed over the years. I'd always been very much 'one of the lads', spending a lot of my time in the local cricket club. The most notable thing which changed immediately was that I stopped swearing and greatly reduced the amount of alcohol that I drank. My attitude to cricket changed more gradually; at first I would go to church on a Sunday morning then, if there was a match in the afternoon, I would play cricket. This slowly changed to the point that I stopped playing cricket on a Sunday because it interfered with church. If anybody had ever told me that one day I would prefer going to church rather than playing cricket, I would have had a good laugh at them.

We went to church as a family and I got more and more involved, helping in the Sunday School and youth work; it was and still is a very important part of my life. I now had a peace in my life that I hadn't experienced before. I used to think that being a Christian must be boring, but it isn't; you still have your ups and downs but life is definitely more satisfying. Christine was happy for me to go back offshore and it lasted for ten years until tragedy struck again.

7

WORKING FOR OCCIDENTAL

I went back to work on the Ninian Southern platform for my next trip and told my colleagues about my new beliefs. At first they thought that I'd grown two heads but we continued to get on well and work well together and my new-found faith soon became fair game for the constant banter that went on between us all. There was a good sense of camaraderie amongst the men on the platform; we all learnt to give and take, to help each other out and laugh together. We all had our own little foibles, which we respected, but also enjoyed winding each other up about.

We worked long shifts whilst we were offshore and, after showering and eating, there wasn't much free time to fill. We played table tennis, pool and darts but this had to stop at 7.00 pm, as the recreation room doubled as a cinema. I preferred its use as a games room, as most of the films were absolute rubbish and the language in the cinema was very colourful. The language was colourful all the time and you had to put up with it but, when it came to watching films, I did have a choice and I usually opted for an early night with a book or a newspaper.

It was an exciting time for the operations team on the platform when the first oil was produced. We had spent a lot of time learning all the production and process equipment and getting it all to work, so producing the first oil and exporting it by pipeline to the Sullom Voe oil refinery on the Shetland Islands gave us all a big buzz. There was lots and lots of complicated and expensive equipment and everything worked well except for one piece of equipment, the flare ignition system, which never worked. There were two flare stacks on the two corners of the oil wellhead area but they were only ever used in isolation, depending which way the wind was blowing. When we were producing oil one of them was always lit as, when you produce oil, you also produce gas.

As we started production all was going well and the flare gas was being routed to the correct flare to be burned, but the ignition system wouldn't work and we couldn't light the flare. The principle of the flare ignition system was similar to that on my gas barbeque at home, which never worked well either, though obviously a bigger version. Much as we tried we couldn't get the flare to ignite. At the time it wasn't a major problem, as the gas was blowing away from the platform and we were miles from anywhere. Had the wind changed, it would have been serious and we would have had to shut down.

At this point Jerry, the Production Supervisor, produced a flare pistol and box of cartridges and we lit the flare by shooting a distress flare through the cloud of gas. Despite several attempts by the maintenance department, the ignition system never ever worked and we continued to use the gun and distress cartridges throughout my time on the platform.

The construction and installation continued and, over the next few months, the water injection and gas compression systems were commissioned and brought into use. It was a busy time but, as all the process equipment gradually came into use, the work pressure eased off. As long as all the production equipment was operating as it should, the work schedule was relaxed, especially on nights. We would take an hour for our meal break and as many coffee/tea breaks as the routine work allowed. If things weren't working as they should we would all pull together and work hard to get everything functioning properly. When the oil production system was down we didn't even get a meal break, but thankfully that wasn't very often.

At the end of fourteen days offshore, having worked eighty-four hours each week, we were very glad to go home and relax. The trip home was eagerly anticipated and the sound we all dreaded was that of the foghorn, which sometimes heralded the cancellation of the helicopter flights and meant extra days on the platform. Any extra time on the platform was paid as overtime but we would lose our time off, as our return dates were fixed. If we were delayed on the platform the relief crew was in Aberdeen, waiting to fly out, and had technically started work at their check-in time.

Christmas came around again very quickly and I was due to be offshore again on Christmas Day. When I'd returned to work after Daniel's death I had asked the Production Supervisor if I could go home a couple of days early at Christmas and return early to make my time up. He'd agreed without hesitation and assured me I could have the time off on compassionate grounds. I had offered to use my holiday but was told that wasn't necessary. As Christmas approached and I went to see him to arrange the time off, reminding him of his promise, he told me it was out of the question as our shift was down to minimum manning; he denied his promise and accused me of trying to emotionally blackmail him. Although his name was Red McCormack, after this incident I used to call him 'Tom' after the famous cartoon character, as the opposite Superintendent was called Jerry, both of them being Americans. When he discovered why, ie that Jerry was the clever cartoon character whilst Tom was the one not to be trusted, I had to drop his nickname and steer clear of him as, in any fall out between us, there would only be one winner – and it wouldn't have been me.

Going back to work for the Christmas trip was the closest I came to packing it all in. Usually a day or two before I went back to work, I would be rushing about and doing all the things that I should have done in the previous twelve days and not looking forward to being away from home. Leaving home for this Christmas trip was a lot more difficult than usual and, when I got offshore, the time really dragged and I was upset. Christine was struggling at home as Christmas Day approached and Rachel was excitedly looking forward to Christmas Day and her birthday, oblivious to the distress of her parents. As a family we have always enjoyed Christmas but, as you can imagine, it has never been the same and still isn't. I counted the days whilst I was offshore and was very pleased when I finally got home.

The Ninian Southern platform was a lot more modern than the Piper Alpha; from the control room you could see what was happening by the instruments and computer feeds and the production processes could be controlled and electronically measured, in contrast to the control room on Piper. The daily production was calculated at midnight and measured in cubic meters but, because oil is priced in barrels, the Americans only talked about production in barrels. Jerry, the Production Supervisor, would ring each night just after midnight wanting to know how much oil we'd made that day. We used to tell him how many cubic metres of oil we had produced and he would then roar "How many barrels?" We always had the conversion figure ready for him, ie cubic metres to barrels, but enjoyed winding him up. I can still picture him now, chewing on his big cigar and roaring at us in his Texan drawl; he reminded us of the Texan sheriff, J. W. Pepper, from the James Bond films. Jerry was an old-fashioned oil man and you couldn't help but like him. As long as the oil went down the line and his American newspaper, the Herald Tribune, arrived on time, he couldn't have given a toss about anything else.

The months rolled by and Christine and I settled into the routine. I really liked the shift pattern and looked forward to my time off. In the two years I worked on the Ninian I can't recall any major incidents, no spills or fires, no explosions and thankfully nobody injured or killed. It was a well-run platform and, with the benefits of hindsight, I wish I'd never left.

I wasn't actively looking for another job but, after chatting with a neighbour (Joe Lynch) who worked on the Piper Alpha on my way back from the shops one day, I discovered that his wages and conditions were better than mine for the same job, though the seven-day-on-seven-day-off shift pattern didn't appeal to me, as it meant doubling my travelling time to and from Aberdeen. However, about the same time I visited Rachel's school to be told that her behaviour, and therefore her work, were affected by my long absences. As the teacher put it, "I can tell whether you are at home or not by Rachel's behaviour". After discussing it with Chris, we decided that I would try to get a job with Occidental on the shorter shift cycle to see if Rachel would be more settled. Losing Daniel had obviously affected her, even at her young age.

Joe got me an application form and I applied, to be told that there weren't any immediate vacancies. However, a few weeks later they phoned, asking me to go to Aberdeen for an interview. It was a proper interview this time and I was told that I had the job there and then. I worked my notice and went straight offshore for them, no induction, no training and their attitude was, "You said you can do the job and we are the best payers in the

North Sea offshore industry so get out there and do the job we're paying you to do".

Working on Piper Alpha was a culture shock compared to ICI and the Ninian; although production had only started three years earlier than on the Ninian it felt like going back to the Stone Age. The well head area was like a jungle, with pipework everywhere and, when you entered, you could hardly move. The platform was smaller than the Ninian but had just as much equipment and, as I've written elsewhere, I was shocked by the lack of control from the control room.

On a positive note, I was on the same shift rota as Joe and travelled up and down to Aberdeen with him. He was very helpful in showing me around the platform and the process equipment. The shift I joined was made up with a good set of experienced operators and they were very helpful and the shift had a good team ethos. The men were interested in photography and we all took photographs of our holidays and home lives and had a genuine interest in each other's lives. In some ways that makes it harder when I think about those who were lost in the disaster, as I felt I knew their wives and children and could imagine the devastation they would have felt. I was allocated a room in the new accommodation block, which had only been lifted onto the platform a few months earlier and, when I saw the original accommodation that the drilling and construction crews lived in, I was very pleased that I, along with the other Oxy personnel, lived in the new block. The facilities in the accommodation block were very similar to the Ninian platform and the food was also plentiful and of an excellent quality.

My only niggle was my roommate, an older guy who was on the same shift as me and who smoked. I could put up with his smoking during the day when we were awake but he would light up in the middle of the night when I was asleep, which was very annoying – and against regulations. It was a strict rule that you were not allowed to smoke in your bed because of the fire risk. The cabin was about eight feet square so we both ended up stinking of smoke, though at least I showered! I went to see Jim Guest, the Deputy Superintendent, to ask him to have a quiet word with my roommate, rather than putting in an official complaint and causing trouble. Jim had previously been a shop steward at ICI on Teesside and had recently been promoted to management; the phrase 'poacher turned gamekeeper' comes to mind with Jim. He told me in no uncertain terms to stop rocking the boat, reminded me that I was still in my six-month probation period and said, "If you don't like it, you know what to do". I soon discovered that comment was a very common reply if you moaned to management and our response to it was "Keep laughing and take the money".

I did know what to do, so I just put up with it and swapped rooms whenever one of my Oxy colleagues was on holiday, earning myself the nickname 'the Cuckoo'. After a couple of years there was a chance to change my rota day from a Tuesday to a Thursday, which I grabbed, as it meant I would have to change rooms and get a new roommate. Smoking problem solved, but the irony of the shift change meant that I now went home on a Thursday instead of a Tuesday. The 6th July 1988 fell on a Wednesday so, instead of being at home the day before the disaster, I was on the platform when it happened. I saw enough smoke that night to last me a lifetime. I got a new room and a new roommate, an operator on the opposite shift called Brian Kirby. We got on well and respected each other's space, making a joke of our differing smoking habits.

I soon settled into the one week on and one week off shift pattern and Rachel settled down at school. It's difficult to say how losing her younger brother affected her; they were close in age, were good pals and had played together well. I didn't think much about it at the time but Rachel had to adjust to it, as Chris and I did, and she clearly missed her brother. Chris preferred the new shift pattern and I soon accepted the extra travel up and down to Aberdeen. We all enjoyed the more settled family life and the weeks and years passed by. I was well paid by Occidental, which helped to compensate for the extra travel, and they were very generous with our phone time; we could phone home every day for as long as we liked. I have harped on a bit about our phone time but the daily (more if needed) phone calls home were precious moments for all of us. From a company perk point of view, against a relatively low cost, Oxy could not have given us a better perk.

After Daniel was born Chris and I decided that our family was complete and we hadn't planned to have more children. However, after he died our plans changed and we desperately wanted more children and were very fortunate to have two more. In 1981 we had a new addition to our family; a little girl called Hannah Elizabeth, who was born on 28th February 1981, quickly followed by a son, Paul Geoffrey Daniel, on 17th April 1982. We were both overjoyed when they were born, as was Rachel who, at the grand age of ten when Paul was born, took to being a little mother, as well as big sister, to both of them. Chris looks back and reflects that Rachel was more help than I was when they were both babies.

I was working on the Piper when Chris was expecting Hannah. Her due date was whilst I was offshore so I went to see the Production Superintendent (nicknamed Mr Pastry, but only people as old as me will remember him) and asked him if I could put in a week's holiday for the next trip, thus giving me three weeks off and hopefully covering Chris's confinement. There was no statutory paternity leave in those days. He sat at his desk, turned to the leave chart, checked the manning and refused point blank. I tried to plead a special case but he would have none of it and warned me to make sure I turned up for the next trip – or else. Fortunately, Hannah was born during my week off so I returned to work like a good boy.

The situation the following year when Paul was born couldn't have been more different. I had been transferred to the Claymore platform, as they were short of operators. I was only there for three months and the work was very similar to that on the Piper; I was the operator on turbine duty most of the time I was there, as they were exactly the same models as on Piper. My time on Claymore was memorable for two reasons; Paul was born on 17th April 1982 and the Falklands war was at its height.

Paul was born on a Saturday and I'd been working nights. Our accommodation was directly below the platform helideck and we were constantly woken by the helicopters landing and taking off when trying to sleep after a night shift. At about 10.00 am, the Production Superintendent, Jim McAllen, came into the room and I could hear a helicopter on the deck above us. He said, "Your wife has started in labour, you are off on the next chopper". As I sat up in bed and started waking myself up, he rushed back into the room and said, "I've told the Pilot to wait, be quick and you can go off on that one". I was out of the bed in a flash and on the helicopter in minutes. The comparison of two people's attitude to a very similar situation was remarkable. Mr. Pastry was oblivious to my personal situation when on the Piper, whereas Jim McAllen couldn't have been more accommodating. It reflected the attitude of Americans to their personnel compared with the British attitude, which was a lot more sympathetic. The only thing that seemed to matter to the Americans was how much oil we made.

The other outstanding memory from my time on Claymore was the morning of 28th April 1982. The night shift Control Room Operator used to finish work about an hour before the shift change-over, take the production figures to the superintendent's office and then wake up the day shift. One morning Gordon, who was an ex Royal Navy Sub Mariner, woke us with the shout, "They've just sunk an Argie cruiser". We woke up to the news that the General Belgrano had been torpedoed and sunk by a Royal Navy submarine. He and a few of his ex-Royal Navy colleagues were very 'gung ho' about such things. However, looking back at the situation, three hundred and twenty-three sailors were killed that day, who would have had people who loved them and have 28th April 1982 etched on their minds, like 6th July 1988 is on mine.

Shortly after my stint of work on Claymore my second eldest brother, Alan, and his family emigrated to Australia. It was a day of very mixed emotions for the whole family and one which has stuck in my memory. I can still see Alan, Val and their two children, Susan and David, outside our house in June 1982 as if it was yesterday. Alan dropped his car off at our house as I was buying it off him and they were driving to Heathrow in a hire car. Paul was a babe in Chris's arms and Hannah was fourteen months old. There were lots of tears, hugs and kisses from the six oldest of us and then they left; they had a plane to catch and a new life to start. The rest of us stayed in the Teesside area and continued to see each other regularly. John, the eldest, also worked offshore; he worked for Chevron on the Ninian Northern platform. Sadly, he died of cancer in 1988 so Mam buried two of her children as well as her husband before she passed away in 2001, which was very hard for her – and all of us, as we were a close and loving family.

8

DISASTER UNFOLDS

The sea was calm and blue as morning dawned on 6th July 1988. It would be a pleasant summer's day in the North Sea. I retired to bed as usual at the end of my night shift. It was a regular day, or so I thought. There were men doing maintenance, the oil wells were flowing, the machines were running, exporting oil, injecting water and compressing gas; it was a hive of activity. The production log for 6th July, the platform's last day, recorded an export of 138,294 barrels of oil, worth $1,936,116, plus gas and condensate.

There were several vessels in the seas around the platform as I headed to my cabin. Two of the vessels, the Lowland Cavalier, positioned twenty-five metres off the south west corner of the platform, and the Tharos, a Multi Support Vessel, anchored five hundred and fifty metres off the west face of the platform, were there to assist in laying and fitting the Chanter pipeline and riser. The Maersk Cutter, a small supply vessel, was about a mile away and the Silver Pit, a converted trawler, was four hundred metres off the north-west corner.

The Silver Pit was the platform's stand-by boat. We used to watch the stand-by boats sailing round and round the platform. There was always a boat on duty, twenty-four hours a day, three hundred and sixty-five days a year. The boats would protect the platform's safety zone from other vessels, only allowing authorised vessels into the zone. It was also there to rescue people from the water, usually a rare occurrence, but later that night it turned out to be a lifesaver. We used to watch the stand-by boats bouncing about in the sea at the height of bad weather when the waves would reach seventy to eighty feet high. Sometimes it would appear they were standing on end in the rough seas and me and my colleagues would comment, "Whatever happens on here, you would never, never, ever get me on one of those little boats". How wrong we were, and how thankful I was to be dragged aboard the Silver Pit later that night. I owe a huge debt of gratitude to all of the crew on board.

Work was ongoing in fitting the new pipeline riser on to the platform to carry gas from the Chanter to Piper. On 3rd July, to accommodate work on the gas conservation module, Piper Alpha switched to Phase 1 gas production. In Phase 1 production the gas recovery system was not as efficient as usual and more gas was burnt off, rather than being exported, though oil production continued as normal. As a result of the switch to Phase 1, the volume of gas flared off each day rose from between one to five million standard cubic feet, to up to thirty million cubic feet. The effects were felt on the platform and there had been an increase in the number of complaints received in the previous few days regarding gas smells.

One of the maintenance tasks being carried out on the platform was the examination and re-certification of each of the three hundred pressure safety valves (PSVs) on Piper Alpha. The work had been ongoing since January and there were just a few PSVs left to check, one being PSV 504, which was located fifteen to twenty feet above the floor of Module C in the midst of a maze of pipes, valves and cables. Its purpose was to open automatically should the substance (condensate) inside reach a pre-set pressure level, allowing a safe means of escape to the flares and preventing any dangerous build-ups. PSV 504 was fitted to condensate injection pump A.

There were two condensate injection pumps, A and B, which were the means by which condensate, which is derived from liquefying gas, was piped into the main oil line and then exported to the refinery, which was located on Flotta, one of the Orkney Islands. Condensate, known as LPG (liquid petroleum gas) by the lay person, is a volatile and highly flammable liquid. It's available for sale in variable sized bottles and is used on gas barbeques, fires and as a main source of gas for people not connected to the National Grid. On the rig, it condensed at a pressure of seventy-eight atmospheres, forty-five times the pressure of car tyres. In normal production both pumps ran twenty-four hours a day.

At 7.45 am on 6th July Bernard Curtis, the Production Superintendent, issued permits for the day's maintenance work. The permit-to-work was a formal, written system which controlled specific tasks to ensure that any potentially dangerous work was carried out with the appropriate safety measures, and that relevant staff members knew of work being undertaken. There was a strictly enforced rule on the platform that no-one could carry out work without a permit. It was one of the safety systems in place to protect the two hundred and twenty-eight men who were living in close proximity to the volatile fuel. At the end of the shift the worker had to return the permits to the control room staff to sign off, stating whether the work had been completed or suspended until the following day. The permit-to-work system had been found to be flawed on previous occasions, most notably following the death of Frank Sutherland, a rigger who had died as a result of injuries sustained whilst working on the rig in September 1987. On this day, the flaws proved to be disastrous.

Whilst I slept two PTWs were issued for work on condensate pump A, one at 7.45 am for routine maintenance on the pump. (This work was never started.) As the platform was liquefying less gas than usual, production could continue with just one pump. A second permit was issued later in the day for work on its safety valve, PSV 504. The two permits were filed in different safety boxes, as the pump was in one area of the platform, the 68ft level, and the safety valve in another, the 90ft level, and PTWs were stored in different boxes for different areas of the platform. They should have been cross-referenced. Having filed the permits, work on the pressure safety valve was started but not completed during the day shift.

Two blank flanges, which were intended to protect the flange seals that were open on both sides of the pipework once the safety valve had been removed, were put in place and secured with stud bolts. They were secured to prevent any escape of hydrocarbons and to prevent any dirt entering the pipework. A blank flange could be used to seal a pipe but, before the pipe could be used, it would need to be checked, pressure-tested and signed off by production staff. As pump A was electrically isolated and couldn't be used without the replacement of PSV 504, the flange wasn't tested. As the end of the day shift was approaching and there wasn't time to complete the work on the pipeline, it was decided that the rest of the work would be undertaken the following day and the PTW was suspended until then.

At about 5.15 pm I reported for my final night shift and, in the handover by Raymond Price, the daytime Control Room Operator, was told that there was nothing out of the ordinary to report. He brought me up to speed on the oil, water-injection and produced water plants as well as the diesel pumps and JB turbines. The gas plant wasn't included in our handover, as it was the prerogative of the Phase 1 Operators who kept a separate log to the control room log, so there was no mention of any work on PSV 504.

In addition to monitoring the processing equipment, there was a considerable amount of paperwork to complete on a night shift. The production figures were kept on a midnight to midnight basis and most of the data was on twenty-four hour charts, which were removed and replaced at midnight. I expected to be very busy from midnight onwards as, on a good night, the 'sheets', as we called them, took about four hours to complete, barring interruptions. There had been occasions when I or my colleagues had been finishing off the paperwork after the shift should have ended.

Following the handover, my shift started as hundreds before had done; I started pre-preparing the sheets as much as possible, alongside chatting with the lads and consuming large quantities of tea and coffee. The mood in the control room was light-hearted and jovial; for most of us it was our last shift before our week off. We chatted about our plans and hopes for the coming week, little knowing what the following hours would bring.

At about 9.30 pm I left the control room in the hands of Bobby V. (Shift Supervisor) and went to phone home to speak to my wife, a part of our nightly routine. After speaking to Chris, I returned to the control room at about 9.40 pm and everything appeared calm with the equipment functioning well. After chatting for a few more minutes, Bob put on his helmet and left to walk around and check the plant and then phone his wife. I was left in the control room on my own. Five minutes later the sequence of events which led to the demise of the platform started. It took just thirty-five minutes, from the first alarm coming into the control room up until the second explosion, the giant fireball that engulfed the platform and was the point of no return for Piper Alpha and one hundred and sixty-seven of the men on board.

It was 9.45 pm when the sequence of events started. An alarm triggered in the control room which indicated that condensate pump B had tripped.

However, there was no means of knowing why from the control room. My role was to convey the message to one of the other operators, so he could go to the satellite control panel situated in the module where it would give accurate information, ie high/low pressure, high/low condensate levels or a mechanical malfunction with the pump. It was then his responsibility to control or rectify the problem. Unfazed at this point, as it was a very regular occurrence, I radioed Taxi Bob (Phase 1 Gas Plant Operator) and informed him. Bobby V. also acknowledged the call on his radio.

Two minutes later another alarm sounded, the JCP panel alarm this time; the JCP panel was the satellite control panel for the condensate system. Again, I called Taxi Bob and he acknowledged the call. I checked with him that he had unloaded the gas compressors, in order to reduce condensate production, as the problem indicated by the JCP panel alarm would most likely be a high condensate level in the condensate collection vessel. The platform was still producing a small amount of condensate and, as the pumps were not exporting it, there would be a potentially dangerous build up. Asking Bob the question felt a bit like teaching your Granny to suck eggs, as we were all experienced operators, but the correct procedure had to be followed.

The condensate injection pumps, which 'spiked' the condensate into the main oil export line, were the platform's 'Achilles heel'. From an equipment point of view, we had four main oil line pumps and only needed to operate with three, we had three source water pumps and only needed to operate with two, we had three water injection pumps and only needed two and we had three gas compressors and only needed two. However, we had two condensate injection pumps and needed both in normal operations. On a bad shift, it was the condensate pumps which kept us busy. I had known them to trip up to twenty times in one twelve-hour shift and I was beginning to wonder if this was going to turn into a 'bad shift' for all of us, and especially for Taxi Bob.

There was only one pump running at the time, as condensate pump A was with the maintenance department. Although the production of oil and gas had been cut back to allow the single pump to cope with the condensate being produced, pump B would have been running at or near full capacity so a fault needed attending to quickly. The rig was continuing to produce some condensate and if we didn't get a condensate pump started we would have to stop the gas compression and flare all of the gas. That was a situation we did our best to avoid.

About five minutes later Bobby V. came back into the control room and said, "We can't get the pump started. I'm taking pump A back from maintenance, as they haven't started on it yet. Get Clarky on the tannoy and we'll get the permit signed off." Clarky (Alex Clark) was the night shift Maintenance Supervisor. As far as we, the Operations team, were concerned there was only one live permit for condensate pump A, allowing the maintenance department to perform PPM (planned preventative maintenance) on pump A, rather akin to a car service.

Bob Vernon checked the work permit and confirmed that the scheduled maintenance hadn't yet started. He and Clarky signed off the permit, thus signing condensate pump A back into service to take over from the broken pump. Clarky asked me to tannoy for Jim Savage, the maintenance electrician, but he didn't respond. We assumed he was in the accommodation block, as he had been working over and finished his overtime at 10.00 pm.

We had two buttons in the control room to operate the tannoy system. The first button broadcast the message to all the production facilities and would only be heard by people who were on duty on the platform. The second button, which had a cover to stop it being used inadvertently, broadcast your message everywhere on the platform, including the accommodation block and people's cabins. The Control Room Operator was not popular when he used this button and woke everyone up but, on this occasion, I had no choice.

I tannoyed for Jim to contact the control room and woke everyone on the platform in the process. He was in the accommodation block and contacted the control room immediately. Clarky confirmed to him that the permit and electrical isolation tags had been signed off and asked him to reconnect the electrical supply to the pump. Procedure allowed only an electrician to do this. Taxi Bob, Bobby V and the other operators were preparing pump A, to start it as soon as they could after the electrical power had been re-instated. They would have started to pressure the pump up; it ran with a suction pressure of about 400 psi.

Soon a new problem presented itself. A single gas alarm sounded, a low gas alarm on C centrif compressor, warning of a small gas leak on the deck above the pump. I accepted the alarm and radioed the information to Taxi

Bob, who acknowledged the message. Another couple of minutes passed and the fire and gas panel went ballistic. Numerous gas alarms for C module all came in together, low gas alarms and high gas alarms, the panel was flashing like a Christmas tree and I couldn't silence the panel, which had a loud klaxon alarm. The quantity and severity of the alarms coming in was unique. I had never seen so many gas alarms activate together before and I barely had time to think; with mounting horror, the realisation that there was a massive gas leak in C module began to dawn.

If you look at the picture of me on page III; that is where I was standing at this point, but facing the other way, at the fire and gas panel. I was trying to accept the alarms and silence the klaxon with my left hand, holding the radio mic in my right hand and trying to talk to Taxi Bob when the first explosion happened at 10.00 pm. I found out later that a flash of blue flames had shot out from below the platform. Captain Michael Clegg, who was aboard the maintenance vehicle, the Lowland Cavalier, which was stationed just twenty-five metres from the south west corner of the platform, saw the explosion. It was felt throughout the platform; men carrying drinks in the accommodation block had their cups shaken from their hands and, in the galley, food and plates crashed to the floor. The control room was a complete wreck.[3]

---

3   For a detailed factual account of the disaster and events leading up to it see Appendix 1: Statement from G. Bollands to Occidental Management following the disaster.

9

ESCAPE FROM THE INFERNO

I found myself on the control room floor in a dazed condition, about fifteen feet away from where I had been standing only seconds before. It was unusually quiet except for the JB generator alarm, which was still going off.

An unusual silence had descended on the normally noisy platform and the room was full of grey smoke. All I can remember is coming round, laid on the floor and my hip was very painful. The control room was filled with smoke apart from the two or three feet just above the floor. I crawled under the smoke and hit the big red button, the emergency shutdown button. It was what I was trained to do and, at this point, I was operating on 'automatic pilot'. I didn't know what to think.

The platform shut down, the main oil and gas lines and the rig's huge electricity generators all stopped and the klaxon on the fire and gas panel was finally silent. The emergency lighting was on and I could hear somebody moaning. It was Alex Clark, who had been standing on the other side of the control room and, like me, had been hurled to his left in the explosion. However, whereas I had been flung into space he had been hurled into the entrance door bulkhead and now lay on the floor, dazed and with an injured shoulder. Ian Ferguson, one of the Oxy fitters, came into the control room and helped him out. As we later recollected the events we joked that,

"Alex Clark was laid on the floor moaning, but that was not unusual for our maintenance department!".

The area where I was standing when the explosion happened was a complete mess. The explosion came through the bulkhead (the one to my left on page III) and destroyed that end of the control room. The fire and gas panel and all our communication systems were in that area; the telephones, the platform tannoy system, the operations radio station, the emergency sailor radio, the communication system to the Claymore and Tartan platforms and the pipeline terminal to Flotta on the Orkney Islands, all unable to be used. The control room, which didn't control much before the explosion, was now totally out of action. As there was nothing else that could be done or communicated from the control room and because of the density of the smoke, I left, breaking the glass on the remote fire alarm hoping it might activate the alarm, but it didn't. Struggling to walk because of my hip, I stumbled out of the control room, which had been my main place of work for the past eight years.

As I left the control room and headed along the outside walkway, I had two main concerns. Firstly, the platform alert hadn't gone off and the deluge system wasn't working because the fire and gas panel had been so badly damaged in the explosion. Secondly, and more seriously, both the emergency fire water pump and the standby fire water pump were on manual and would need to be started at the pump in D module. The fire water pump not being allowed to start automatically was standard practice on the platform when diving operations were taking place, the procedure having been put in place a few years earlier. There had been a serious incident when a pump started automatically whilst a diver was in the vicinity of the pump suction, which was very dangerous for the diver.

The procedure was that, before diving operations started, the Diving Superintendent would ask the Control Room Operator to complete a 'pump status form'. The form would show the operating status of each of the pumps with suction direct from the sea. The pumps that were on standby were switched to the off position in the main electrical switch room by the Control Room Operator, who was then not allowed to alter the status of the pumps (ie start or put on automatic) without the permission of the Diving Superintendent. That night the Diving Clerk, Ed Punchard, had come to the control room for the pump status form, which I completed. I then switched the pumps to off, signed the form, Ed countersigned it and I kept a copy for the file. That was why I was so concerned; we had a major incident and no water for the firefighting equipment.

I was shocked by the sight that greeted me outside. There were a number of people milling about, mainly dive personnel who had come up to the main production deck, known as the 90ft level. They had nowhere to go and the fire and smoke were frightening. There was a large oil fire coming out of B module and the wind was blowing the flames back on to the platform around the crane pedestal, cutting off the walkway in that direction. The smoke from the fire was like a black wall cutting back across the platform. You could have cut the smoke with a knife and we instinctively knew that we would be committing suicide by going into it, thus cutting off our escape in the other direction.

I found Bob Vernon and Erland Grieve, from the production team, and Robbie Carroll, the Safety Officer, on the deck, all equally shocked and dazed. I explained that all the communication systems were out of commission, that the alarm had not activated and that we must get the emergency diesel fire pump in D module started. At this point we all knew that the situation was serious but we still expected to be able to deal with it. In 1984 there had been an explosion and fire on the platform upstairs in the Phase 2 gas module but, on that occasion, the fire and smoke were blown away from the platform, all the emergency facilities were fully operational and the non-essential personnel were evacuated by helicopter. When this incident happened, I was on my week off and the Oxy staff coined the phrase "If we have an incident out here, I want to be on my week off, but if I am on the platform, I want to be up and about, on shift, definitely not in my bed". The saying, which was coined a bit tongue in cheek, turned out to be very true. Out of approximately forty Oxy staff on the platform only six of us survived, four of whom were on the night shift and the other two up and about working overtime.

The fire water pump could be started in several different ways and was always tested by the day shift control room on a Sunday morning. It could be started remotely at the fire and gas panel then at the pump, by the platform power system, a separate battery pack, a pressurised gas system or by a falling pressure in the fire ring main.

It was the Control Room Operator's job to start the pump, but I couldn't as my hip had been injured in the explosion and I was struggling to walk, never mind put on the heavy breathing equipment. Bob Vernon and Robbie Carrol both put on breathing apparatus and went into the black wall of thick smoke to try to start the emergency fire water pump; that was the last time I saw them. Seeing the two of them disappear into the smoke is a memory that is etched on my mind. It could - should - have been me but my minor injuries saved my life. At this stage, none of us could have imagined what was going to happen in the next ten minutes.

Erland spotted that my left thumb was spouting blood. He told me to raise it above my head and apply pressure to it and, as he wrapped a filthy handkerchief around it, I remember commenting, "I'm not going to die from blood loss, but septicaemia is a distinct possibility!" It was a lighter moment in a very serious situation.

The situation was getting worse, the fire was getting worse, small explosions were going off and we knew that urgent action needed to be taken. We were surrounded by smoke and flames, trapped ninety feet above the water. The flames blowing back from B module blocked one route and the thick smoke stopped us going the opposite way. If we could have, we would have headed up the north side of the platform, which was the route back to the accommodation block. This was our muster point and getting back to the accommodation block would have enabled me to inform the emergency teams of the situation. However, it was fortunate that the smoke stopped us because the accommodation block proved to be a horrific death-trap.

There was nowhere else to go but down. One of the riggers tied a rope to the handrail and people started climbing over the rail and down the rope - going over the handrail and climbing down a knotted rope was not something I would normally entertain, but desperate times call for desperate measures. I put on a life jacket and went over. The descent was extremely difficult; I was very fit in those days but, even without my injuries, I would have found it difficult. The descent was arduous and space on the rope was in short supply; the rope had knots in it and my life jacket kept snagging on the knots in the rope and I had to keep dragging myself back up to free it. I managed to get to the bottom and on to the spider deck; there was no choice as the person above me kept sitting on my head.

The Silver Pit, the platform's stand by boat, which had had its red hull and white deck freshly painted a few days earlier, came as close to the platform as was safe and launched the Zodiac rescue craft, which started evacuating people off the platform. The Zodiac was on its third rescue run and was against the platform leg. There were two small spaces left on the boat and I managed to scramble down the leg and into the boat, closely followed by Neil Cassidy, who was a contract tiffy working the night shift with the Oxy crew.

The Zodiac pulled away from the platform and headed west towards the Silver Pit. It had only been sailing about a minute or two when we stopped, about seventy or eighty yards from the platform, due to engine trouble; it was 10.20 pm. There was a second explosion and a massive fireball totally engulfed the platform. Thankfully the wind blew the fire and smoke away from us but the heat was intense. I was shielded from the worst of the heat by the Coxon, but Neil, who had climbed into the boat behind me, felt the full strength of it and his overalls began to combust.

Looking back towards the platform, the scene behind us was terrible. There were lads jumping off the rope, falling off the rope and jumping off the platform from the 90ft level with their clothes on fire. It was horrific. I saw one of the men fall from near the top of the rope and bounce off one of the protectors around the platform leg. I thought, "poor fellow, he's had it". However, I'm pleased to tell you that I met him later and he'd survived, albeit with burns and a broken back.

Thankfully the engine sprung into life and we were able to move away from the platform towards the Silver Pit. We reached the Silver Pit and I was dragged aboard by my lifejacket, as I couldn't climb up the rope scramble net. The heat radiating from the burning platform was tremendous, even at the relative safety of the Silver Pit, which was several hundred yards from the platform by now. I felt desperately sad as I looked back towards the platform and thought of my friends and colleagues who were still aboard and wondered who, if any, would survive. I hadn't seen Sandy or Gordon, who were both working in B module, since the alarms started coming into the control room, nor Taxi Bob, who was working in C module, where the first explosion was. I'll never know for sure, but I think it's safe to say that they would all have been injured or killed in the first explosion, as they would have tried to get back to the control room if they could.

The crew on the Silver Pit were excellent. They did their best to look after us and the rescue craft went back to the platform looking for survivors. Somebody bandaged my thumb, which was still bleeding profusely, but I was struggling to walk because of my hip. I felt like a spectator and could do nothing useful, which was very frustrating. We had been on the boat about thirty minutes when cries for help were heard and three men were spotted nearby clinging to floating debris. The captain tried to manoeuvre the boat to rescue them, but the sea swell made it too difficult. Suddenly this 'little' boat, as we had thought of it when on the platform, was now a large boat as it tried to manoeuvre close to the injured men. After several failed attempts to rescue the men, one of the rescued divers who was on board put on a lifejacket, tied a rope to the boat and to himself and went into the sea to affect a rescue, successfully.

The Silver Pit and the Zodiac continued to look for survivors as the fire raged and explosions continued from the platform, which was now in a terminal state. Most of the explosions were relatively small at this point, compared to the massive explosion of the first high-pressure pipeline at 10.20 pm. That pipeline, measuring a yard in diameter, had brought gas from the Tartan platform to Piper at a pressure of 1800 psi (fifty to sixty times the pressure of a car tyre), before being exported to the MCP01 platform. It was that explosion that changed everything and was the point of no return for the platform.

There were two massive explosions caused by more high-pressure pipelines rupturing, the Piper export gas line to MCP01 and the gas pipeline to the Claymore platform. I found out later that the second major explosion, the gas export line to MCP01, destroyed a rescue boat and several men within the vicinity, including two men who were trying to rescue survivors. The third explosion at around midnight destroyed the last pipeline remaining intact, the Claymore import/export line, and caused the platform to split between module A and module B. Within the hour, we watched the platform slip slowly into the sea, leaving nothing except the remains of module A. It seemed to happen in slow motion. A gap appeared between modules A and B, which slowly got wider and wider then all of modules B, C and D slipped slowly into the sea.

It was surreal watching the events unfold before my eyes. It was like watching a disaster movie but this was real life; I had lived and worked on this platform for nearly eight years and knew most of the men on board. The most devastating point was watching the accommodation block, housed at the top of module D, fall into the sea knowing that so many men were still inside. Brian Kirby, my roommate, was one of the many men who were trapped inside the accommodation block when it plummeted into the sea; his body was later recovered by the salvage divers. I felt so sad and couldn't help but cry as I watched. Up until that point, even though the intense heat and smoke would have made survival difficult, there was hope that some would survive. That hope sank along with the accommodation block.

I turned to Ian Ferguson, feeling hopeless, and said, "That's it, the accommodation block has fell into the sea and they are all dead, including Erland." His reply surprised me, "Erland? Erland Grieve is down below in a bunk." He had been one of the three people rescued from the floating wreckage by the diver earlier in the evening. I went below as fast as my injury would let me and was shocked by the state he was in. He was in agony; his hands and face were just big scabs, like crisps. There was no morphine available and it was clear that there were men down below who would die if they weren't transferred to hospital quickly.

I went up to the bridge of the boat to speak to the skipper, who was busy steering the boat and continuing to look for any survivors. When I asked what was happening to the badly injured men below, he replied that it was his duty to stay on station and look for survivors. I was so frustrated. I pointed out that there wasn't much point rescuing men from the sea and then leaving them to die in agony and that he had at least two men below who were likely to die soon without expert medical help, along with a number of other injured men.

At this point he called Rescue 1, the RAF Nimrod aircraft which was co-ordinating the disaster response. They replied and, when the skipper informed them of our situation, asked for our position and Rescue 138, one of the search and rescue helicopters, called us. The skipper told me to get the aldis lamp out of the cupboard, which I then plugged in and flashed it out of the window. After a few minutes Rescue 138 located us. The skipper took instructions from Rescue 138 on where to steer the boat, well away from the platform and heading into the wind. Once we were in place Rescue 138 lowered a winchman on board. A number of seriously injured survivors, including Erland and a Frenchman called Eric Brianchon, were rescued and taken to the Tharos, where an emergency treatment facility had been set up, before evacuation to hospital in Aberdeen. Erland survived but unfortunately Eric died a few days later in Aberdeen Infirmary.

I had hoped that the rest of us would quickly follow them to the Tharos but that wasn't to be. I was still on the bridge with the skipper when a hatch at floor level behind us opened and a 'wee boatman' with a heavy Peterhead accent said, "You are going to have to shut the engines down as that leak on the diesel fuel pump is getting worse and there's diesel sloshing about all over down here." At that point, I must admit that my thoughts were very selfish, along the lines of, "I can't believe this, I've managed to get away from that disaster and now I'm stuck on this boat with a serious fault and the potential for another fire!"

After several survivors had been winched off the Silver Pit, the captain sailed about four miles east and upwind of the burning platform to enable the engines to be shut down and repaired safely. The platform was several miles away but the massive blaze lit up the whole sky and the plume of dense black smoke stretched over the horizon. There followed several hours of frustrating drifting in the North Sea until the diesel leak was finally repaired and the boat got back under way and continued its search for survivors.

At about 6.00 am, after spending about eight hours on the boat, it was my turn to be winched off, as I was deemed unfit to climb aboard another rescue boat. By now I was so desperate to get off the Silver Pit that swinging high above the North Sea in a harness didn't unduly worry me, and I was taken to the emergency medical facility on the Tharos. It's amazing how little things stick in my mind that remind me of that night of 6th and 7th July. My abiding memory of being in the rescue helicopter was being given a small pack with a drink, biscuit and chocolate bar. I drank the juice, then looked at the carton and the sell-by date was fifteen months out of date. At the time, it was the least of my worries but every time I see a sell-by date it reminds me of that fateful night.

10

RETURN TO TEESSIDE

The rescue helicopter took me to the emergency medical facility on the Tharos, where they cleaned my thumb and put a proper dressing on it. Again, different and strange memories stand out. My two abiding memories are watching Dr Strachen do his fitness regime in front of the other medical personnel and being asked for my name, address and telephone number for the fifth time. I'd been asked for the same details firstly by a member of the Silver Pit crew, then the Diving Clerk on the Silver Pit, the rescue personnel who came on board the boat, on the rescue helicopter and now on board the Tharos. Everyone who asked for my details explained that this was to enable the rescue co-ordinators to inform your family that you are safe as quickly as possible; that is ironic, as I will explain later.

Dr Strachen stands out in my memory, as he had come out to the Piper in the last year or two to facilitate medicals for the Oxy personnel. Depending on your age you had to have a routine medical at least every three years. The said doctor told some of the Oxy personnel and wrote in their reports that they were overweight. The last thing you wanted was a poor medical report and no one likes to be told they're fat. They were, therefore, very unhappy and some of them pointed out to him in no uncertain terms that, compared to him, they were like Twiggy! It was bizarre watching him work out and boast about his weight loss, given the circumstances going on outside, but no complaints about him or any of the medical team, they did a great job.

I was then airlifted by helicopter from the Tharos to Aberdeen Royal Infirmary, arriving about 8.00 am. The pale blue sky was glowing pink as the sun rose, echoing in the start of a new day and a new reality for many of the families whose loved ones had worked on the Piper Alpha platform. I was on one of just eleven helicopter flights which ferried survivors back to the safety of dry land in the early hours of Thursday morning. Sixty-four men were airlifted to the hospital, twenty-one of whom were admitted to either the Plastic Surgery and Burns unit or the Accident and Emergency ward. By 7.00 am it had become apparent that there would be no more survivors.

On arrival at the hospital I was whisked into the Accident and Emergency department, where I was sent for X-rays on my hip and thumb. Once again, the obligatory name, address and telephone number were asked for, this time by the hospital staff and the Occidental Emergency Co-ordinator. The Scottish NHS dealt with me well within the four-hour waiting time; in fact, they dealt with me well within a four-minute waiting time.

After being X-rayed I was laid on a trolley, waiting to see the doctor again, when I was spotted by Bill Fleming, a colleague who lived in Aberdeen and who was on his week off, but had come to the hospital to see how he could help. He asked if I was alright and if there was anything he could do for me. I was anxious that my family knew I was alive, as I realised that news of the accident was being broadcast, so I asked him to phone Chris and let her know I was alright. He returned a few minutes later with the Emergency Co-ordinator, a smartly dressed man in a suit, collar and tie, carrying a clipboard. The Emergency Co-ordinator and the Oxy Co-ordinator, who was also with them, told me that they had stopped Bill phoning my wife, as they were attending to informing people, because they didn't want any false information getting out.

Bill asked what I wanted him to do, which was obviously to phone home, so he turned to Mr Clipboard and very forcefully told him where to go! Five minutes later Bill returned, having spoken to Chris and given her the news. This was how she found out that I had survived, despite the endless giving of my name and address and the many phone calls she had made to the information co-ordinators. The only answer that she and the family got back was, 'missing, presumed dead'. I haven't seen or spoken to Bill since that morning but we're both very grateful to him, and I definitely owe him a 'few wee drams'.

I went back in to see the doctor, who had the results of my X-rays. The X-ray showed that there was debris in the gash to my thumb, which she found, removed and stitched the wound. I still have a scar on my left thumb, which I call my 'Piper Alpha scar'. The X-ray to my hip showed that nothing was broken and the doctor said I was very fortunate, as the very corner of my hip bone had taken the blow; had anywhere else taken the impact it would have been a puncture wound. She asked if I had any burns or had inhaled any smoke? I had a few small burns round my neck and had inhaled smoke in the control room but, as I was desperate to get out of hospital and my only thoughts were gratefulness to God that I'd survived and an overwhelming desire to go home, I said I hadn't.

I walked to the entrance foyer of the hospital, where the Oxy representative told me that there were facilities to get washed and changed at the Skeen Dhu airport hotel. However, when I asked him about getting to the hotel he told me that he was too busy to worry about that. I don't know how he expected me to get there. Fortunately, in the hospital's central foyer was a gentleman from the Salvation Army, who had come to help and offered me a lift to the Skeen Dhu.

Also in the foyer was a police officer who had a list of survivors. I was number sixty-four on the list and, when I asked how many had survived, he said it was sixty-four.[4] It was just after 10.00 am on the 7th July. I knew there were between two hundred and twenty and two hundred and thirty men on board. I wasn't sure of the exact number but I knew nearly all the beds were taken, as one of my colleagues who slept in the cabin next to me was on holiday and a contractor had been using his bed. As the number of personnel on the platform increased, the last beds issued to contractors were the beds usually occupied with Oxy staff; as we had permanent beds, unless the platform was full, our beds remained empty. The maths of the situation was not difficult – about two hundred and thirty on board, minus sixty-four survivors, equals approximately one hundred and sixty-six missing, presumed dead. It was now about twelve hours since the incident had occurred and we were taught at our survival training that you couldn't expect to survive in the North Sea for more than thirty minutes. I nearly collapsed with the shock; it was the first time the enormous scale of the lives

---

4   Unfortunately Eric Brianchon died a few days later in hospital, making the total
     number of survivors sixty-three.

lost hit me. When I confirmed how many men were likely to be missing it was the police officer's turn to be shocked.

As I walked out of the hospital I was taken aback at how many TV and press people were there. Alistair Burnett thrust a BBC microphone in my face and asked me what had happened. I beat a sharp exit! The Salvation Army man was very protective; he took me to his car and drove me to the Skeen Dhu. He was equally shocked and distressed when he realised how many men were missing.

I limped into the Skeen Dhu airport hotel in my dirty overalls and rig boots, looking and feeling very conspicuous. It was a long, fifty-yard walk from the front door of the hotel to the reception desk and all heads turned. I must have looked as bad as I felt, which was dreadful. I'd been awake for nearly thirty-four hours, was unwashed, unshaven, wearing dirty overalls, dirty boots and a big bandage on my hand yet the receptionist asked me, 'Have you a reservation, Sir?' I was approximately the thirtieth survivor to turn up at the hotel, yet was asked the most banal question!

I replied that I had been told there were washing facilities and a change of clothes here for survivors from the Piper Alpha platform. An older, and more sensitive, receptionist overheard and quickly intervened, telling me where to go. When I got to the room I met Harry Calder, who had already washed and changed. We greeted each other with a hug and I asked him how he had escaped.

He recounted how, after the first explosion and subsequent fire, everyone had gone to their muster point, which was in the galley, situated directly under the helideck. At that point things were relatively calm, as some of the men had been on Piper during the 1984 explosion and all non-essential personnel had been safely evacuated by helicopter on that occasion. The men were talking amongst themselves, getting drinks and speculating about what had happened. He said that nobody knew anything, as no contact could be made with the control room or any of the on-shift production personnel; all they could see were the flames and the smoke.

However, as the minutes slipped by, people were becoming more and more distressed by the lack of information, the fire, which was getting worse, and the amount of smoke which was starting to ingress the galley. Harry said that some of the contractors were starting to leave the galley, despite the instructions by Occidental management to remain, which was the emergency procedure. Eventually Harry decided to try to escape himself, as he knew his way around the platform well. He left the galley, going outside into the heat and choking smoke, and started climbing down to the 68ft level, which was where he was when the fireball engulfed the rig at 10.20 pm. At that point he had no choice, so jumped off the flaming rig into the cold waters of the North Sea. Fortunately, he was uninjured, was quickly picked up by a rescue craft and taken to a supply boat.

There was an outside line in the room so I immediately phoned home and spoke to my sister, Hazel. She was so pleased to hear my voice and confirm to the rest of the family that I was alright. Whilst talking to her, the doorbell rang and it was two police officers, calling to inform them that I had survived but they didn't know anything about my injuries, as I was in the Aberdeen Royal Infirmary. Hazel shouted through to tell them that I wasn't, I was on the phone talking to her! They said that they were very pleased and wished everybody well, very grateful to leave with a positive outcome after such a traumatic night.

Hazel told me that my wife, Christine, and brother, Mike, had left immediately after finding out that I had survived from Bill Fleming and were on their way to Teesside airport to get a flight to Aberdeen. My oldest brother, John, who worked for Chevron on the Ninian Northern platform, was getting ready to drive to Aberdeen with my mother, as they thought I was still in hospital in Aberdeen. I told Hazel to stop them, as I was definitely coming home. After speaking to my eldest daughter, Rachel, and other members of the family I ended the call and went to get a shower. Hannah and Paul, who were seven and six respectively, had gone to school. They hadn't been told what was going on and were a little bemused at Grandma and all their Aunties and Uncles being in the house when we weren't having a party.

I got a shock when I walked into the bathroom; it was the dirtiest bath I had even seen, more black than white. Having a bath was out of the question but I did manage to shower and then wash my feet in the sink when I got out of the bath. I had to put back on the clothes which I had worn all night, but there were clean overalls and boots to put on over the top. I felt very conspicuous in the bright orange overalls when I returned to the reception area and was quickly approached by the police and taken to a large hall, which was a buzz of activity. There were lots of people being questioned and men in suits walking around with clipboards, trying to look busy.

Before giving the police my statement I asked an Occidental staff member to check that my wife and brother were on the Teesside flight and bring them to the hotel, not the hospital. I then spent the next hour or so giving the police officer an account of everything that had happened since the start of my shift at 5.15 pm the previous night. When I told him the number of men who had been on the platform and the number on the list of survivors I had seen at the hospital he too was very, very shocked.

The interview had hardly finished when an official from Aberdeen Council, carrying the obligatory clipboard, approached me and demanded a statement of events. When I refused, he got a bit shirty and said that he would get the police to make me. I directed him to the police officer who had just taken my statement and said he could have a copy of that, which I would sign, but that was all he was getting out of me. I managed to avoid him for the rest of the time I was there.

After what felt like an eternity, the Oxy representative came and told me that Christine and Mike were on the flight from Teesside and would be brought straight to the Skeen Dhu. When we were reunited it was a very emotional moment for all of us. I have to admit that Chris and I shed a few tears, but just little ones.

By this time the world's press had descended upon Aberdeen and, although most were still at the hospital, I was an easy target in my bright orange overalls. Fortunately, Chris had had the foresight to bring a change of clothes for me so I quickly got changed and blended into the background, becoming just another guest at the hotel having a cup of tea and sandwich with friends.

I was desperate to go home and the Oxy rep booked the three of us on the next available flight back to Teesside. As we had a few hours to spare, he also arranged transport to and from the hospital for us, as I wanted to visit some of the other survivors, especially Erland Grieve. However, the hospital wasn't allowing any visitors and, despite pleading a 'special case' I got nowhere. However, I did bump into Colin Lockwood, who had been the night shift Lead Operator the previous night, finishing his shift at 6.00 am on 6th July and returning home to Dundee that day. I also met John Slaymaker, who had travelled up from Devon to see what was happening and see his colleagues.

Chris, Mike and I returned to the Skeen Dhu where the Oxy rep had flight tickets ready for us and arranged transport to the airport; I really appreciated his help. At the airport, I was just another passenger but it felt surreal to be sitting in the airport bar having a drink and waiting for a flight after all that I'd experienced in the past twenty-four hours.

The flight to Teesside was uneventful. I kept a low profile, as I had at Aberdeen airport, and avoided the small press contingent, which was waiting when we landed. I did speak to a lady from Radio Tees as Christine and Mike said that they'd been very supportive of my family during the previous, very anxious night as they waited for news. The first my family had heard about the disaster was on the 11.00 pm Radio Tees news, which Hazel had heard as she was driving home. She had phoned the radio station for confirmation and more information and they had shown great sympathy and kept them updated throughout the night, a very different response than that from the official phone centre. It was 6.00 pm when I returned home to a very joyful reception from the entire family.

11

LIFE AFTER PIPER

Looking back to the days, months and years after the disaster has a surreal feeling to it now and it's difficult to time everything accurately, as different events and incidents all seem to merge together in my memory. This is unusual for me because my memory is normally very good. I'm naturally a talker and I didn't have any problem talking to people about what happened; in fact my local doctor encouraged me to talk about the disaster and I am still talking about it nearly thirty years later, the main difference being that when I talk about it now I don't get as upset as I used to. The tears are a lot less frequent, in fact now just about dried up.

After getting home on the 7th July, I was overjoyed to see the children and the rest of my extended family and I thanked God that I had survived. Some of my fellow survivors struggled to come to terms with the fact that they had survived when so many had died, but I didn't, I was just very, very thankful. From the moment I was dragged aboard the Silver Pit and watched the horrors unfolding before my eyes, I classed myself as being very fortunate to be alive, and to have sustained such minor physical injuries compared to some of the other lads, who had serious injuries and burns. I did have psychological issues, which I had difficulty coming to terms with and which presented challenges to my family and friends.

Eventually everybody went home and I was shattered so went to bed; I'd been up and about and awake for over forty hours. Considering how tired I was, I didn't sleep well and kept waking up and shouting at the nightmares and vivid images which kept flashing through my mind. Poor Chris didn't get much sleep either and the next morning she carted me off to the doctors and I was given some medication and sleeping tablets. I slept better after this, but the nightmares were still there, as vivid as can be. In the end Chris moved in with one of the children so that she could catch up with her rest.

Unlike me, in fact in direct contrast to me, Chris doesn't like talking about the disaster and wishes that everybody would shut up and forget about it. Her trauma at the time was very different to mine and she still remembers the stock answer of 'missing, presumed dead' which she believed to be true for six hours after hearing about the accident. Obviously I knew I was alive and at no point did I expect to die, but Chris's experience was very different. In addition, my behaviour and my refusal to get any counselling help still wrangles with her. It is to her credit that we are still married today; some survivors' marriages didn't survive.

In the early days things didn't get easier. I was glad of the medication but I wasn't happy taking it, as I didn't want to become dependent on tablets. The doctor prescribed sleeping tablets and 'happy pills' which, after discovering from Chris that they were antidepressants, I decided not to take. The sleeping tablets were helpful at first and I managed to wean myself off them after a few months. My local doctor, Dr Leigh, was excellent. He was very patient with me and gave me a lot of time. Without me realising what he was doing, he just kept encouraging me to talk, to him and everybody else. My first five-minute appointment with him lasted over an hour, as I described the disaster to him in detail and I felt very sorry for the waiting room full of people I walked through on my way out. I went back to see him again the following week and the visit took a similar pattern; this time he encouraged me to talk about how Oxy were treating me and how Christine was, rather than the disaster itself. The third meeting, a fortnight later, focused more on how I felt and how the children were.

The meetings were fortnightly, then monthly, though he encouraged me to book an appointment any time I wanted. He asked me several times if I wanted to see a 'trick cyclist' but I refused, telling him that there was nothing wrong with me and I was only going to see him to get my sick note renewed. He agreed to write 'anxiety state' on my sick notes so as not to tarnish my medical record. Looking back, encouraging me to talk and share what had happened and how I felt was the best help that he could have given me, and I appreciate his support.

Chris was working as a District Nurse at this time and her employers had told her to take as much time off as needed. I came home on Thursday 7th July and Chris went back to work on Monday the 18th; she couldn't stand being at home with me all day as my behaviour was driving her mad. In the first few weeks the phone never stopped ringing and, when I wasn't on the phone talking about what had happened, I was pacing about our home and garden. I'm told that I couldn't sit still.

The calls were from the press and Oxy management in Aberdeen. I got a lot of calls from the press but fortunately they weren't camped out on the doorstep like they were at the homes of other survivors. We'd moved to a new house nine weeks earlier so the reporters all went to my old address, which was only about a quarter of a mile away, and the new residents simply told them we'd moved but they didn't know where to. Unfortunately, I hadn't changed our telephone number, so they persistently rang that.

Oxy management called a lot and their calls all followed a similar pattern. After asking how I was, the concern was always followed by questions about the platform. I soon realised that they were more interested in finding out information to protect their safety record and prepare to defend themselves at the public enquiry, rather than concern for my health and, when my answers changed to "I don't know" or "I'm not sure", the calls soon stopped.

I had a lot of visitors in the days after the disaster and one has always stuck in my mind. It was Friday 8th July and the front doorbell rang at about 4:00 pm. On the doorstep were two young girls aged about thirteen. One of the girls checked that I was Geoff Bollands and then explained that she was Brian Kirby's niece. She asked if I had seen or heard anything of Uncle Brian, as they hadn't heard any news about him and nobody could give them any information. It was a very sad moment, as I couldn't tell her anything. Brian, who had been my roommate for several years and who was a really nice lad, didn't survive and his body wasn't recovered until the accommodation block was lifted from the bottom of the sea, months later.

Another incident which I can recall as if it were only yesterday happened the following day. It was Saturday 9th July and my daughter, Hannah, was out playing. We had only lived in our new home for nine weeks so we didn't know our neighbours well. Over the fence at the bottom of the back garden there was a grass play area and Hannah was playing out there with another little girl called Dawn, whose house was on the other side of the play area. I was pottering about in the back garden and Hannah shouted to say that they were going to play in Dawn's house. About half an hour later I saw Dawn's mother dragging Hannah across the grass and telling her off.

Before I had the chance to open my mouth, she started telling me how naughty Hannah was because she had been telling lies and she wasn't going to let her play with Dawn again. Through her tears Hannah protested her innocence and I asked Dawn's mother to explain. Her explanation went something like this, "The two of them were playing nicely together in the house when the news came on about that terrible disaster on the oil rig when all them poor people were killed and Hannah said that her Dad was on that. I told her that it was very naughty to tell lies like that but she kept repeating it, so I've brought her home and I think that she needs a good talking to". You can imagine her face when I confirmed that Hannah was telling the truth and she started apologising to me most profusely. I said that it was Hannah that needed the apology, not me.

I didn't realise it at the time, but I was suffering from PTSD[5] and, like the doctor, Chris kept suggesting that I get some professional help, which just annoyed me and apparently made me worse. The first time I heard the expression PTSD was in 1991 during the Gulf War when the papers started writing about the soldiers who were suffering with health issues when they came home. As I read and heard accounts of how they had reacted and their families' descriptions of their behaviour, I realised that was me. I'm not a very patient person at the best of times and I'm told by a lot of my friends and family that I was impossible to live with at this time. Looking back, friends, family and people at church were very patient and considerate with me for, which I have thanked them and would like to thank them again publicly.

Technically I was on the sick and continued to be paid by Oxy, but I went up to Aberdeen on numerous occasions at the request of Oxy Management.

---

5   Post Traumatic Stress Disorder (PTSD) is an anxiety disorder caused by very stressful, frightening or distressing events. Someone with PTSD often relives the traumatic event through nightmares and flashbacks, and may experience feelings of isolation, irritability and guilt. Cases of PTSD were first documented during the First World War but the condition wasn't officially recognised as a mental health condition until 1980. (https://www.nhs.uk/conditions/post-traumatic-stress-disorder-ptsd/)

I was glad to go up as I used to go and see Erland in hospital. On the 18th July I was formally interviewed by three of Oxy management engineering staff. A transcript of the interview is included in Appendix 1. It is a blow by blow account of what happened for the more technically minded.

It was good to visit survivors in hospital when I was in Aberdeen and I also attended a number of funerals of friends and colleagues who had died in the disaster. I found the funerals very, very distressing and, after Harry Flook's funeral, which I found particularly upsetting, I vowed not to go to any more. I'd worked side-by-side with Harry on the same shift team for nearly eight years. He'd worked on the Piper longer than me and was always willing to help and pass on the benefit of his experience; we got on well together and I liked and trusted him. We used to joke amongst ourselves that, working twelve hours a day together, eating together, spending leisure time together and, on the odd occasion, sharing a room together, we spent more time with each other than we did with our wives and families. He'd recently swapped shifts and was on days on disaster night, so would have been in the accommodation block when the pipelines exploded.

I found the funeral very sad and then afterwards we went back to their family home. Harry was a cockney, ex Royal Navy, and they'd moved up to Monifieth, near Dundee, with the job. All of Harry's family and friends were there and they were so upset. It was heart wrenching and, as I shared with their grief, it dawned on me that 'there but by the grace of God' it could have been me. All these bereft people could have been my wife, children, Mam, brothers and sisters. I felt their grief intensively, but not the raw grief that they felt as a family. I came out of their house in tears and was very pleased that I had my friend, Terry Outterside, who took care of the long drive back to Teesside.

Nearly thirty years later I would be telling lies if I said that I think about it every day, but certain things always remind me of specific people who were involved with the disaster. I'm always reminded of Harry when I see a Chelsea Pensioner, as his Dad was ex-army and the family had been trying to get him into the Chelsea Pensioners. Harry was so pleased when he was finally accepted. Every time I see a Chelsea Pensioner on the television or in a picture I think about Harry and wonder how his dear old Dad felt when he heard of the accident.

I didn't go to any more funerals after Harry's, except one, that of Alan Carter who lived less than a mile away from me in Middlesbrough and whose wife I'd visited when I realised he hadn't survived. They recovered Alan's body out of the accommodation block and, unfortunately for Alan, it was his positive attitude to work that meant he was on the platform on the 6th July. He was a Shift Supervisor and should have gone home on Tuesday the 5th but volunteered to stay on the platform to help with the production facilities during the day shift.

Looking back, stopping going to colleagues' funerals is another decision in my life that I regret. Straight after the disaster I was all over the place going to every funeral that I could, as I felt it was my duty to go. I coped with them quite well, just quietly being there and keeping myself in the background and going straight home after the church service. The experience I had at Harry's funeral, when I went back to his family home, really upset me and it was the last one I attended, apart from Alan's.

The accommodation block was finally recovered from the bottom of the sea on 15th October 1988 and the bodies of eighty-seven men were recovered. Some of these men I knew well and I feel that I should have had the guts and shown the respect that my colleagues deserved by attending their funerals. I particularly regret not going to Brian Kirby's funeral. The only excuse that I can make is that I was suffering from PTSD, even though I didn't realise it at the time. I did visit Brian's wife and apologised to her afterwards and she was very gracious and forgiving to me. It's easy to make excuses for myself, but I did suffer from some vitriolic abuse from some of the deceased families. However, I also was shown a lot of love and affection from other families. Looking back, I made some strange decisions after the disaster and I don't and have never felt anything but sympathy towards the bereaved. None of us know how we would react after a tragic disaster.

On one of my regular trips back to the Oxy offices in Aberdeen, a few months after the disaster, Alex, who was an Office Administrator came into to see me. "Geoff" he said, "I've got something for you" and much to my surprise, he gave me thirty pounds. I wondered what he was doing; he then gave me a couple of credit/bank cards and my driving licence. (See photo on page IV) I was confused and asked him how he'd got hold of the items, to be told they'd been recovered from my wallet when they had lifted the accommodation block from the bottom of the North Sea. After my initial confusion, I was amazed that the items had survived the intense heat and then three months submerged in four hundred feet of water. It was a poignant moment, and a reminder of all those men who hadn't survived.

On one occasion I was visiting Erland in hospital in Aberdeen and the nurse asked me to go and sit outside whilst she did what nurses do. I was sat in the corridor outside his room when a doctor walked round the corner who spotted my bandaged hand and quickly put two and two together; he asked how I knew Erland. When I told him, he sat down and asked me how I had survived and then gave me some startling news. He said that he had just come from seeing a number of men who had jumped from the Piper helideck and survived. The helideck was one hundred and seventy-five feet above sea level (Nelson's column is one hundred and sixty-nine feet high, to give a perspective). All the medical professionals were amazed that these men had survived and had very few injuries, the worst being broken bones and some bad burns.

I went to see them there and then. They were what we called the 'Geordie Scaffolders'; they were employed by a company called Deborah Scaffolders, who had just been successful in gaining the contract to work on the Piper. It had been their very first trip to work on the rig so I hardly knew any of them, but it was so good to see them and I asked them how they'd escaped.

Billy Clayton, who was the Foreman, told me that they were just going to bed when they felt the platform shake. There was a bit of a commotion outside in the corridor; people saying that there had been an explosion, so he and his squad went up to the galley, which was their designated muster point. They had been there a while and he said that nobody knew what had happened and that they were all told to stay in the galley. The situation was getting worse, smoke was ingressing the galley and he could hear a helicopter flying around. He wasn't impressed with the organization, or lack of it, so he and his squad went outside and up on to the helideck. The smoke was bad but the heat from the fire was bearable; he wasn't sure what to do next but had a faint hope that the helicopter would pick them up. Suddenly there was a massive explosion and fireball (which I refer to as the second explosion at about 10:20 pm). The heat became intense and their overalls were beginning to smoulder and their skin was burning, so they jumped off the helideck, all one hundred and seventy-five feet of it.

I said what a very brave decision it had been to jump off the helideck and Billy replied with these words that I will always remember, "Bravery had nothing to do with it. We had no choice; it was a case of jump and try or fry and die". He said that they hit the water with a hell of an impact but the water brought them round and they swam away from the platform and the heat, before being picked up out of the water. I am not scared of heights, but I had once ventured to the edge of the helideck on a clear, windless day and looked over the side. It was a long, long way down to the sea and I quickly stepped back, even though there was a safety net at the edge. Before the disaster it was totally beyond my comprehension that anybody would ever jump off that helideck, which emphasises the extreme heat from that fireball.

I continued to visit Erland every time I went to Aberdeen, which was quite often, and you will be pleased to know that he made a full recovery, albeit a painful one. One part of his treatment was to inject fluid into his neck and, every time that I saw him, his neck was a bit fatter; this continued until it looked like he had a skin-coloured travel collar on. The doctors then drained the fluid out and used the skin to graft on to his face. (I believe that this medical technique was first used after the fire at the Bradford football ground in 1985.) In all his injuries, and the pain and suffering that he endured, I never heard him once complain about his situation and he has my utmost respect, as he went back to work offshore. There were approximately forty to fifty men who worked for Oxy on the Piper and only six survived, four of whom were on night shift and the other two were working overtime. Erland, who had suffered the worst injuries, did go back to work offshore.

12

THE CULLEN ENQUIRY

The next thing that I had to deal with was the public enquiry, which was chaired by the High Court Judge, Lord Cullen. It was up and down to Aberdeen again for nit-picking and detailed meetings with the company solicitors beforehand. I didn't feel that there was any need for the meetings and the coaching, as I would simply tell the truth; to me what happened is what happened. They agreed with me that it was essential that I told the truth at all times but advised me to just answer the questions and not volunteer additional information. They then asked different hypothetical questions and, depending on my answers, advised me to "just say that" or "there isn't any need to say that". I was told that all the help and coaching they gave me was because they were interested in looking after my interests. I wasn't so sure whose interests they were looking after.

The enquiry started in April 1989 and I was given a time slot on a Wednesday but told to be in Aberdeen on the Monday morning in case I was called early. Chris came with me to Aberdeen; I wasn't looking forward to what I saw as an ordeal and she was looking forward to it even less. We both sat in court all day on the Wednesday listening to lots of technical evidence, which I found quite interesting, but which went straight over Chris's head. I started giving my evidence as the first witness on the Thursday. Looking at all the barristers and the legal teams was very intimidating; there were teams representing the UK government, the TUC, Occidental, contractor companies and others I can't remember. I did feel a little anxious and nervous but there was no need and I soon relaxed, as Lord Cullen wasn't allowing any aggressive behaviour by the legal teams to any of the survivors. In fact, they all handled us with a great deal of sympathy.

I was on the witness stand for the full day and went through all the events leading up to the disaster and everything that happened on that fateful night; how all the routines and permits were issued and monitored. Towards the end of the day the barrister representing Oxy asked me if I had ever ordered that production on the Piper be completely shut down because of a safety concern, a question I was surprised not to have been asked earlier. He knew the answer would be "Yes" and, when I replied, he asked me to explain the circumstances.

The circumstances were that, earlier in the year, I was working on the night shift and was one of the two operatives who were responsible for modules A and B, the oil wellheads and the separation vessels. I was in the control room when a contractor rushed in to say that there was a big gas leak in the wellhead pipe work in A module. I rushed down to A module and there was gas shooting out as visible vapour for about ten feet. The pipe work in A module was a jumbled mass of oil production lines, gas lift lines and water injection lines.

I radioed the control room and spoke to Joe Lynch, told him the situation and asked him to stop all hot work on the platform. I scrambled into the pipe work to try to find exactly where the leak was coming from so that I could isolate the leak and let the line de-pressure. The size of the leak and the high pressure of the gas stopped me getting close enough to identify where it was coming from and, if it had found a source of ignition, it would have been like a huge blowtorch. I then radioed Joe again and asked him to shut production down. He confirmed with me, "Are you telling me to shut production down?" and I replied "Yes". Joe pressed the button and shut production down.

The barrister then made a big point about how the 'highly trained' (his words not mine) production staff had the authority to shut the platform down for any safety situation if they thought it was necessary. He was very pleased with the point that he made to the enquiry about how good Oxy were regarding safety. I then waited for one of those other highly paid barristers to ask me the obvious question, which I think should have been, "What were the results of the investigation into the incident and what lessons have been learnt?", but I wasn't asked the question.

The answer would have been that, after Joe shut production down, the gas leak lessened and the Deputy Production Supervisor and I managed to locate the leak and isolate the gas flow to it. Whilst we were shutting the valve to isolate the leak the deluge went off and that was it, incident over. I explained to the management what had happened and was told to go and get some dry clothes on and return to work. The cause of the leak and my actions were never discussed with me. The leak was from a line that supplied gas to the well heads to help with oil recovery, i.e. gas lift, and the pressure in the line was about one thousand, eight hundred and fifty psi (about sixty times the pressure in your car tyre). After the incident a major modification was made to the gas lift system; a rapid closing shutdown valve was installed in A module, enabling the system to be shut down quickly without affecting production.

I could also have explained that, a few weeks after the incident, I was standing in for the Shift Supervisor when the Deputy Production Supervisor, the same one who helped with shutting off the gas leak, came and sat next to me in the control room and asked why I was standing in as supervisor. The system was, if you wanted to be considered for promotion on Piper, you had to be prepared to accept a temporary promotion without extra pay or your application wouldn't be considered. I replied, "You know the system, if I don't take the responsibility and show that I can do the job, I will never get promoted". He then told me that I would never ever get promoted because of my actions in shutting the platform down without permission and all the other operators had had this pointed out to them, on an unofficial basis.

The official mantra from Oxy was, 'No.1) Safety comes first. No.2) Production comes second. No 3) Drilling comes third.' We always used to have a laugh at this and say, tongue in cheek, "Safety is always the first priority, unless it interferes with numbers two or three." I realised that day that our tongue in cheek mantra was correct but, if we didn't like it, we knew what to do. I often ask myself, after this experience, would I have shut production down on the 6th July, had I had the opportunity to do so. Thankfully it's a question I don't have to answer, as I didn't get the opportunity.

That was the only notable thing that happened to me at the enquiry and, at about half past four, Lord Cullen adjourned court for the day. I asked if I was free to go home and, after just one more question, he let me go, feeling very relieved that it was all over. I was very pleased to read later that Lord Cullen stated on page 84 in his report that, "I consider his account sufficiently reliable and credible".[6]

---

6   Cullen, The Hon. Lord W. Douglas (1990). The public inquiry into the Piper Alpha disaster. London: H.M. Stationery Office. ISBN 0101113102. 488 pages, 2 volumes

13

PLANNING TO GO BACK

It was a relief to get the evidence I was required to give to the Cullen enquiry behind me. I was warned that I could be called back, but I wasn't. The next few years were a strange time in my life and I continued to have emotional 'ups and downs'; thankfully the 'ups' gradually started to get longer and the 'downs' shorter. During all the turmoil and mood swings I experienced at this time, the question that I got asked the most by family, friends and Oxy was "Are you going to go back offshore?" Depending what week and/or mood I was in, they would get a different answer ranging from, "No never" and "I don't know" to "Yes". It sounds bizarre, but that was how I was. After about a year the 'no never' answer slipped out of my vocabulary and I was very much in the 'don't know' state of mind. Obviously, there wasn't a Piper platform to work on and I didn't want to work on the Claymore. However, plans were being made by Oxy for a new platform to replace Piper Alpha, the Piper Bravo platform, which was installed in 1992 and started production in February 1993. The days turned into weeks, which turned into months, then years and I was on gardening leave, enjoying playing golf and cricket, enjoying my time with the family and actually doing some gardening.

I now realise that I enjoyed the time with my family more than they did, as, apparently, I was driving them all mad. It's hard for me to describe what suffering from PTSD felt like because, from my point of view, I was OK; there was nothing wrong with me. My family's experience was very different and, when Christine used to challenge my behaviour or lack of patience, my reply was always the same, "There's nothing the matter with me, it's you ... it's the children ... it's somebody else's fault." My perspective at the time was that it was everyone else who was argumentative and confrontational. I now realise that I was very short-tempered and would fly off the handle about the most stupid things, but I couldn't see it at the time. In retrospect I can see much more clearly the effect my behaviour had on the family and I regret not taking Christine's or the Doctor's advice to seek professional help. Family and friends have all said since that I was very difficult to live with whilst I was still employed by Oxy and uncertain what to do about returning to work. As soon as I made a clear decision, there was a dramatic change in me and I was quickly back to my normal self.

There was another big court case that I had to attend at the Scottish High Court in Edinburgh, between insurance companies who were fighting over who paid who what. I was determined not to go, resisted all the persuasion from Oxy and was prepared to accept the consequences for my actions. As I've said before, this was a spell in my life when I wasn't at my most rational. Eventually I was made to see sense by a friend who was a solicitor, who warned me that they would issue me with a summons and, if I ignored the summons, an arrest warrant would follow. Dragging all the pain of the disaster back up again and answering questions to legal teams who weren't interested in the truth, only in winning for their client, was something I had to do. However, every cloud has a silver lining and I discovered that Erland was also due in court, so we managed to arrange our appearances on the same day and enjoyed a good night out in Edinburgh after a lousy day in court.

The support from my doctor and my family and friends continued during this difficult period of time. The Pastor and friends from church were very patient and supportive of me, also encouraging me to seek professional help, but sticking with me when I refused and was difficult. Although I didn't realise it at the time, the church had put a strategy in place to support me. I received a lot of one-to-one visits from individuals and just thought people were being nice, but it was a plan designed to help me. I was also made a focus for prayer from the local, national and international church without knowing it. Had I known, I suspect I would have very ungraciously responded that I was fine and didn't need any support. The leaders suggested that I take some time off from my Eldership duties whilst I recovered, which

West side of Piper Alpha. Prior to the disaster; top left is the helideck and in the middle of the platform is the crane pedestal, where the first fire was situated.

The remains of Piper Alpha.
'A' Module is being held up by the oil wells that had been drilled into the ground.

1980s version of me in the control room. The fire and gas panel is directly behind me and the bulkhead to my left was destroyed in the explosion. The impact of the explosion hit me from that direction.

My driving licence, after being exposed to the fire and spending
three months at the bottom of the sea.
Still in remarkably good condition.

IV

The Bollands Eight in 1961. Taken on my oldest brother's wedding day in 1961. Left to right: John (oldest), Hazel, Anne (the baby), Trevor, Michael, David, Alan, Me.

My family. Left to right:
Hannah, Christine, Paul, Me and Rachel
We all have our family ups and downs, and I am
eternally grateful to all four of them for supporting me.

Daniel Geoffrey Bollands (1974-1978)
Our special little boy.

Three special grandchildren. Left to right:
Daniel, Hugo and Elizabeth
I am so grateful that I am here and able to enjoy spending time with them.

was met with my usual response of, "There's nothing the matter with me". I remember one specific occasion when I stormed out of an Elders' meeting arguing that everyone else was wrong except me. They were very patient and forgiving towards me and, looking back, it was definitely me that was out of order. My faith in God strengthened during this period of time; I was extremely thankful that I'd survived and being part of a church family gave me the security I needed at the time, and has continued to do so since.

Two friends in particular stand out, Terry Outterside, my best friend from amongst my offshore colleagues, and Brian Goodall, who I first met when I worked at the Gazette in 1969. Terry was a Production Operator with Oxy and I met him on my first shift on the Piper in 1980. He lived in Stockton-on-Tees, a few miles from me, and we shared a common interest in playing squash and used to meet every Friday when we were both home to play, often twice a week when my shift rota changed. Our wives also got on well together, so we would often go out for meals with each other. Terry was transferred to the Claymore platform about a year before the disaster but still worked the same rota as me and always classed himself as very lucky that he wasn't on Piper on the 6th July, as he would most likely have been killed along with his ex-colleagues.

After the disaster we continued to meet regularly to play squash and socialise together. Terry was one of a very unique group who supported both Middlesbrough and Sunderland football clubs; it's virtually unheard of in the North East to be classed as both a 'smoggie' and a 'mackem'! I eagerly looked forward to Terry coming home, as he was a reliable contact to Oxy and life offshore. He had all the latest news, official and unofficial, about what was going on with the company and my ex-colleagues and, after our squash game, it was twenty questions. It's difficult to quantify it, but the oil industry and working offshore still felt a big part of my life.

I'd known Brian for about nineteen years and we used to go to watch the Boro together; Chris and I also went out regularly with Brian and his wife, Jeannie. At the time of the disaster Brian owned a very successful company, Heritage Hampers, which became the sponsors to Middlesbrough Football Club in seasons 1988/89 and 1989/90. Brian had seats in the Directors' boxes for both home and away matches and he took me all over the country watching the Boro. I can recall lots of matches but two in particular stand out in my memories from that time.

We'd been to Old Trafford and had been beaten one-nil. Mitch Hatfield, my old boss from the Evening Gazette, was with us and was ranting and raving about the players in the car going home because he felt they couldn't care less about winning. He came out with the phrase, "Don't they realise it wasn't just a game of football, it was a matter of life and death". I brought him up short by saying, "Hang on a minute, we've just lost a football match, that's all. I know a lot about life and death and that had nothing to do with life and death." Mitch, who wasn't known for giving ground easily, reluctantly said that he'd take that from me, but wouldn't take it from anyone else. Sadly Mitch died a few years ago.

The second incident is the most powerful, and the most painful. It was the 15th April 1989 and we travelled to Loftus Road to watch Middlesbrough draw with Queens Park Rangers. I remember the game very clearly but what made it such a notable day were the scenes we watched unfold at the Hillsborough stadium on the television in the Directors' guest lounge after the game. I was completely devastated watching the horrific events and thinking about all those poor innocent victims who had just gone to watch a football match, as I had, and the devastation their families would face. I wrote earlier about the misuse of the word 'devastated'; the families of the Hillsborough victims truly know the meaning of the word.

The question about returning to work continued to sit at the back of my mind but I still couldn't decide what to do. I got regular calls from the Oxy Human Resources Department, usually from a man called Keith Middleton. He didn't put me under any pressure but asked if he could help in any way. We discussed three possible options, a desk job in the office in Aberdeen, working on the Piper Bravo project or going back to work offshore on the Claymore platform. The situation dragged on and Oxy insisted that I went to see a psychiatrist so, following their demand, I saw one twice.

I travelled to St Andrew's hospital in Northampton; I can't remember the psychiatrist's name, but he was a pleasant chap who asked me lots of questions. I told him there was nothing wrong with me and that I was wasting his valuable time and my own. Chris came with me; we stayed in Warwick and had an enjoyable time visiting Warwick Castle but the visit to the hospital was a waste of time. In conversation he mentioned that his brother was the editor of the Middlesbrough Evening Gazette and he was coming to Middlesbrough to see his brother and go to the football at Ayresome Park.

I saw him at the football match and spoke to both him and his brother and, when I went back to see him a few months later, after the usual chit-chat I asked about his visit to Middlesbrough. He said he'd enjoyed his trip but the quality of the football was poor. I agreed with him and said jokingly that watching the Boro on a regular basis was enough to depress anyone.

A few months later Oxy sent me a copy of his assessment, which stated that there wasn't much the matter with me, as stated by me, but I was suffering from some depression that was caused by being a Boro football supporter. You couldn't make it up; all that time, effort and money and he thought I was depressed because I was a Boro supporter. I've been going to Ayresome Park since I was about nine and the one thing that you get very used to is being disappointed with the Boro football performances and results. As to causing depression - half the town would be put on suicide watch if he was correct!

A couple of years went by and I knew that I had to start getting on with my life; I couldn't stay at home on gardening leave for ever. The calls from Keith Middleton at Oxy continued, still without undue pressure. My first choice for going back to work would have been on the Piper Bravo project but Jim McAllen, who had been the Production Superintendent during my time on Claymore and was now the Pipeline and Production Manager (the big boss), wouldn't hear of it. Following the incident on Piper Alpha in early 1988 when I'd shut the plant down, they didn't want someone on Piper Bravo who might shut production down if he thought there was a dangerous situation developing and, after the disaster on Piper Alpha, they would have had difficulty arguing. When I met with Jim McAllen he told me that the only place I was going to go back to was the Claymore platform where, "there was more gas whizzing round than there ever was on the Piper". Those were his actual words.

That made my decision for me; I dug my heels in and refused to go back offshore on to Claymore so my gardening leave continued. The regular squash and update meetings with Terry continued and he kept encouraging me to go to work on Claymore. His arguments were that it had a new accommodation block with two-man rooms, I knew the job and most of the lads and would soon settle into the routine. He felt that it would help me to come to terms with things and, if I didn't settle, I wouldn't be any worse off. In the end, in 1992, I changed my mind and decided that I would go back offshore and work on Claymore. I did discuss it with Chris but by now she was so tired of my mood swings and said, "I'm totally fed up with the whole thing and I don't know why you're asking me because you'll only do what you want." So I did. I contacted Keith at Oxy to tell him my decision and he arranged for me to see the company doctor in Aberdeen for an assessment.

The group of doctors they used for company medicals were called Aberdeen Industrial Doctors, which had been quickly abbreviated by all the lads offshore to the Aids doctors. Aids was a very topical issue in the 1980s and 1990s and we all hoped that their medical skills were better than their marketing skills. Telling Chris that I was going to see the Aids doctor always generated the desired reaction and this time was no exception. The doctor declared me fit for work; he decided that I was neither a nervous wreck nor too gung-ho about the situation and requested to see me again after two trips offshore.

It was all set up and I was due to fly up to Aberdeen and go offshore to the Claymore platform. However, the night before the big day, I couldn't sleep and was tossing and turning all night. Chris put the light on, sat up and asked me what the matter was. I explained that I couldn't settle or sleep and the thought of getting on the helicopter and going back offshore was keeping me awake and distressing me. Chris then gave me the best piece of advice that I have ever been given, "Now you listen to me. I have had enough of this, for the last three or four years you have been driving us all mad and this is what you should do. Firstly, go to sleep, secondly, get up in the morning and phone Oxy first thing and tell them that you are never going back and resign from the company and thirdly, close the book on the disaster and GET ON WITH YOUR LIFE."

I went to sleep, got up the next morning and, at one minute past nine, phoned Keith Middleton and, for the first time in my life, did what my wife told me to do. I resigned on the telephone and put a letter in the post the same day, confirming my resignation to a somewhat relieved Human Resources Manager, who had just had a problem removed from his in-tray. It was like closing a book and starting again. A very different Geoff Bollands started looking for a new job.

14

A DIFFERENT PERSPECTIVE

I've described my experience of the events of 6th July 1988 in detail and have written about the months and years following the disaster from my perspective. However, as I've written previously, what Chris and my family experienced was very different but equally life-changing. It was an experience that touched and changed each one of us and affected relationships deeply. Chris and my two eldest children have shared their perspectives on the disaster and how it affected them; Paul was too young to remember. It's important to realise that the effects of the Piper Alpha disaster, as with any tragedy, reach far beyond those who were directly involved, to their families and friends, and everyone has a story to tell.

Chris writes her experiences:

"I have found the experience of being the wife of someone involved in the Piper Alpha disaster very difficult. We had experienced personal tragedy ten years earlier and, as Geoff has written, only parents who have lost a young child will understand the intensity of that grief. However, Piper Alpha was a very public tragedy which changed our lives again, and also those of hundreds of other families. From the moment I stepped into Teesside airport with Mike on the 7th July to fly up to Aberdeen and was hounded by the press, I realised

that the national extent of the disaster would impact our personal experience. Thirty years later, as another anniversary approaches, that is still the case.

Geoff has written that I don't like talking about the disaster. I don't find it therapeutic in the way that he does; on the contrary, it is a time in our lives which I would prefer to forget. My daughters have both described their memories very eloquently below. For myself, I would sum up the night of the 6th/ 7th July as a nightmare. To watch the horrific pictures of the rig where my husband worked on fire and collapsing into the sea, believing that he was still on board, but not knowing for sure, is any wife's nightmare. The frustration of not being able to find out any definite information, to simply be told that he was 'missing presumed dead' compounded the agony of the situation. I watched the events unfold on the TV at home surrounded by Geoff's family and some friends from church. His elder brother John, who worked on the Ninian Northern platform, commented that it must be very serious when he saw the Chinook helicopters on duty. Looking back, I can't describe how I felt other than a sense of shock and numbness, almost as if I wasn't there and was watching somebody else's life unfold.

Geoff came home the following day and life changed from that point on. The next few years were extremely difficult. It was clearly a painful adjustment for Geoff, who was ill, though he wouldn't acknowledge it or seek help. For me it was a desperately lonely period of time as I sought to support Geoff and the children, who were all affected by the disaster in different ways. I had no close family of my own and, although people at church were kind and tried to help, they didn't really know how to support me, and I didn't feel able to ask or be completely honest about the difficulties at home because I didn't want to be disloyal to my husband.

Geoff's personality changed; he was aimless and would wander around the house like a lost soul, he became aggressive and argumentative, taking his frustration out on me and the children, and could be unpredictable at times. There are a number of incidents which I can remember clearly, of which Geoff has no memory. We were in B&Q one day, shortly after the disaster, and the tannoy went off. Geoff panicked, he became very agitated and physically dragged me out of the shop; the tannoy had obviously triggered a very painful memory, though he wouldn't have been able to recognise it.

To make matters worse, I had to deal with hate mail, which was delivered by hand to our house. I shielded Geoff and the children as best I could and passed the letters directly to the police. We also experienced abuse when we attended the Memorial Service at St Nicholas Church in Aberdeen on 20th July 1988, when the mother of one of the victims approached us and was very abusive.

I went back to work as a District Nurse, which gave me another outlet and helped me to cope with the challenges at home, though I have to admit there were times when I didn't want to go home at the end of my shift. Without my faith and the sure knowledge that God was with me, I don't think we would have survived and be where we are now – but we did and we're still together thirty years later. The Piper Alpha disaster is an experience which we all still carry with us, whether we talk about it or not; it affected each member of the family and life has never been the same since."

Rachel, my eldest daughter, was fifteen at the time of the disaster and she can still remember that night vividly. She writes:

"When you are fifteen, you think you know it all and believe you can handle whatever life throws at you. However, the adage of 'I wish I knew then what I know now' rings very true to me now.

I was living with my family in Nunthorpe. We had recently moved to a new house; my Mum liked to move, which I find funny now as I think it's a pain, having moved around myself several times. I had, and still have, a 'little' sister Hannah and 'little' brother Paul who were both at junior school. I was going through the testing time of sitting my GCSE exams at Nunthorpe Comprehensive School. We were the first year to participate in the new style of GCSE exams, so the pressure was on. I didn't particularly like school, but I worked quite hard – if I didn't I would have had to answer to my Dad! But, he knew me well when it came to motivating me; he had set me a sliding scale of financial rewards depending on how well I did with my exam results and I am pleased to say it worked.

Dad was due back from work the following day so the weekly shift in discipline was about to occur. As children, we knew that Dad coming home meant we wouldn't be able to 'get away' with as much as we did with Mum. Dad had a strong sense of discipline so we would be, or at least try to be, on our 'best behaviour' for him. But in saying that, we all knew we were very much loved as a family.

That evening I would have gone through the normal routine of a fifteen year old girl, spending at least half an hour in front of the mirror and putting off going to bed as much as possible. The next thing I remember is our front door bell ringing. I mentioned we had moved to a new house; well it was actually a bungalow and my bedroom window looked out over the front door.

It was around 5.00 am but it was light and sunny, so I got out of bed and looked out of the window. The doorbell went again, and my Mum had woken up. I heard her ask "Why is the milkman ringing the doorbell?". I looked out of the window and saw that it was one of Dad's brothers, Uncle Mike. "It's Uncle Mike, Mum" I said. "Oh ok" she said and off she went to answer the door. At this stage I didn't think it was strange that Uncle Mike was at our front door at 5.00 am, and then it all changed.

I was still in my bedroom when Mum answered the door, but my bedroom door was open and I was putting on my dressing gown. "Hi Mike, come in" Mum said. Uncle Mike responded by saying something to Mum which I couldn't make out but then I just heard my Mum make a noise that I will never forget. It was like she was trying to breathe in as much air as she could in one breath and it seemed to go on forever. I went into the hall and Mum was crying in Uncle Mike's arms. "What's wrong" I asked. "Your Dad's rig has been on fire all night, Rachel, and your Dad's missing" he replied.

I learnt that my Aunty Hazel, one of Dad's sisters, had heard the news that Piper Alpha was on fire on the radio very late the previous evening. She had contacted some of the family and they decided to watch events unfold and see if they could establish what had happened to Dad before coming to wake Mum up. For that I am thankful – imagine sitting through that night watching the oil rig go up in flames not knowing where your father was.

People began to arrive at our house. We put the television on and what was truly happening began to unveil itself in pictures. I can remember standing in what we called 'the little lounge', it was our kids' tv room, and watching the news, thinking, "How will my Dad ever get out of that?"

Hannah and Paul got taken to school by Uncle Mike. We still smile about it, as he had a Jaguar then, which was quite swanky, but the big thing was he had dared to park in the staff car park, which was a huge no, no. The reason he did so was to speak to the staff to let them know what was going on. Hannah and Paul thought he was quite a rebel; some might say he still is!

The day seemed to go in slow motion; more people arrived from our family *and close friends from the church we went to. We kept calling the number but couldn't get an update; by this time I believe it was nearly lunch time.*

The turning point came when the phone rang – it had rung almost constantly all morning, but this turned out to be a very different call. One of the lads who was based in Aberdeen had gone to the hospital where the victims had been taken. My Dad, at this stage was in hospital. He'd seen my father who had asked him to call us to let us know he had made it off the rig and, even though he was injured, he was alive.

Mum took the phone and the message was relayed – Dad was alive and in the hospital. Mum asked, "Is he burnt?" but didn't get an answer. The phone went dead. A few minutes later the phone rang again, it was the same chap. He apologised saying, "I am sorry Chris, it's just so over-whelming" or words to that effect. "No, Geoff is ok, he's injured but OK".

What a joy to hear my Mum say those words.

Action stations kicked in – Uncle Mike was taking Mum to the airport and they were going to Aberdeen. At the time there was a huge court case going on in Cleveland, so the airport and the flight were full of journalists.

It's only recently that my Mum shared with me what happened at the airport and on the flight. Journalists picked up that Mum was flying to Aberdeen for only one reason, to be with someone from Piper Alpha. Mum told me that while they were trying to get flight tickets sorted, journalists were trying to ask her questions. She said she tried to 'hide' behind a pillar. My Mum is quite a shy person and people firing questions at her in a state of shock and bewilderment would have been her worst nightmare.

Anyway, it didn't take Uncle Mike long to see what was happening; he had obtained some tickets for the flight, tickets that had already been allocated to some of the journalists. In very simple but straightforward language he suggested that no more questions were to be put to either him or Mum!

They made the flight and Uncle Mike bought Mum a brandy and lemonade with the instruction, "Drink that Chris; it will make you feel better". My Mum did not drink, but did as she was told. Again, she only told me this a couple of weeks ago and the thought of my Mum downing a large drink made me smile. It's probably the only time she has ever drunk brandy! We have a lot to thank Uncle Mike for that day, along with the rest of our family and friends.

I have obviously discussed contributing to this book with Dad, because what occurred to me is that I can't really remember what Dad was like once he finally made it home. I can remember significant events that happened to us as a family, but not what my Dad was actually like. But my Mum can.

Dad was a lost soul for about four years; Mum says he would disappear for hours and no one would know where he had gone. He would wander from room to room staring out of the windows. He was sometimes angry, sometimes vague. He refused to go to the doctor – fortunately my Mum did for support. One of the saddest things about this time, which again my Mum only shared with me recently, was that our family were victims of hate mail. On one occasion a chap came to our door and personally delivered a letter to my Mum questioning why my Dad deserved to live.

Throughout this time, it was my Mum who held our family together. The Piper Alpha affected every one of us, in various ways, both mentally and physically. Without Mum and her faith in God, I am not sure we would all be where we are now."

Hannah was only seven at the time of the disaster so her memory of events is limited and very different to Rachel's. She writes:

"On the morning of 7th July 1988 my memory of events is limited, as I was only seven years old. I remember being woken by my Grandma Edna (my Dad's Mam), as it was time to get up for school. Breakfast was ready and, as my brother and I walked through the house to the kitchen, every room was full of family and my parents' friends. When we asked why everyone was here so early, we were told that they had come to see my Mum. I don't remember seeing my Mum or sister that morning, I imagine they just wouldn't have known what to say to us.

Even though I did not know what had happened to the Piper Alpha, I knew that my house being full of people, huddled together and whispering, meant something wasn't right. However, when you are a child you are easily distracted, and I arrived at school thrilled. Paul and I would normally walk to school together, but that day my Uncle Mike drove us there in his Jaguar - this would have taken twice as long as walking! He parked in the teachers' car park and we were allowed to enter through the front door; we were late, but the headmaster didn't say anything. Even though this was all highly unusual, we enjoyed our VIP treatment. It was a normal day at school and, when I got home, my Grandma was still there but my Mum had 'gone out'.

My next memory is of watching the news with my Dad; he had a bandage on his left hand because he had been hurt at work. Watching pictures of the Piper Alpha on fire over and over again, hearing the newsreader talking about men and fatalities, and knowing that my Dad worked on an oil rig, I asked him if he was there when it was on fire. Even though he said yes, I did not understand the enormity of what had happened to him and all the other families involved.

Suddenly my Dad didn't go to work any more. Even though he was at home all the time, I can't remember him actually being there. Often I would see him standing at windows looking out at the garden for a long time. He had always been strict and that didn't change.

Thankfully, my Mum and Dad sheltered us from what had happened as much as they could and it wasn't talked about unless it needed to be. One day I was told not to accept any letters or parcels from the postman. I remember Dad being summoned to court and he really did not want to go. A girl at school told me "You only live in that house because of what happened to your Dad" even though we'd moved there a few months before it happened. It's only looking back that I can see some of the impact that night had on our family life.

I now have a family of my own and I can't imagine how awful that night and day must have been for my Mum and the families of the men who were on Piper Alpha that night."

15

TURNING PAGES

At last I turned the page over and felt so relieved; it was like starting a new life and finally coming to terms with what had happened. I knew what I wanted to do; I wanted to be a financial adviser and I wanted to be independent. I'd always been interested in the stock market and, when I went to work offshore, I had some capital to invest for the first time in my life. I'd subscribed to a couple of investment magazines, researched the investment process and started investing in the UK stock market. The share club on Piper Alpha had encouraged me, as there was a mutual interest amongst the members and we all made positive contributions about what to buy and sell. I enjoyed the 'buzz' I got from investing – and still do.

As a youngster at school I'd enjoyed 'wheeling and dealing' and, as I reached my forties, I became interested in pensions; a bit late, but better late than never. I knew my way around the mortgage market, as I'd had a mortgage from being twenty-two years old. I knew enough about the financial advising and stock-broking business to know that I wanted to be independent. I didn't want to be forced into recommending things to people that I didn't think were right for their circumstances.

I was in a very fortunate position financially. I had received compensation from Occidental, enough to enable me to leave Occidental and take a much lower paid job and study for new qualifications, but not enough to stop work altogether. I received a lot more than many people get for minor injuries, but a lot less than I could have got if I'd gone with the American 'ambulance chasing' lawyers. I was content with what I was offered and decided not to fight for more. I don't know what would have happened if I had fought for more; the added stress could have been the straw that broke the camel's back with my mental health and could have caused our marriage, which was on the brink at times, to break up. God was good to me. I had enough to comfortably bridge the gap whilst I developed a new career and I now have a successful business which provides a living for my son, daughter and son-in-law, in addition to Chris and myself.

I spoke to Dave Abrook, a member of the squash club who had a financial adviser's business in Middlesbrough; he was very helpful and gave me good advice and guidance. It was 1992 and Dave explained to me that, in order to register as an Independent Financial Adviser (IFA), I would have to work for a financial/insurance company for a year and pass the Financial Planning Certificate exams. There were two routes to gaining the one year's experience and Dave didn't think that I would like either of them. The first route would be to work for a direct sales company, who would give me good training in the industry, but the focus would be upon high pressure sales techniques. Dave thought that my investment and pension knowledge would help to get me started; I would be trained and then work on a commission only basis.

The more Dave outlined the role the less it appealed to me. He explained that the training would be at a residential centre and, once I had learnt the basics, I would be required to write a comprehensive list of family, friends and acquaintances who I would then be required to make appointments with to try to pressure them into a sale, using my newly acquired sales techniques. The company wouldn't worry if I resigned because they would have the long list of several hundred of my contacts to work through. It was the complete opposite of how I wanted to do things and the chances of me sticking it out for a year were nil.

The second option, and the one Dave felt would suit me better, was working as an insurance man collecting premiums round the doors and I would receive some training on the job. I soon found a job with United Friendly, working out of their Redcar office. I was assigned a tough area called South Bank, which was essentially a collection of terraced and council houses nestling in the shadows of the steel works. I was glad of the opportunity and doubled up with a trainer for a couple of weeks, who introduced me to my patch and the intricacies of filling in and balancing the weekly ledger.

The job wasn't ideal, but I did gain experience and received some training to enable me to give advice on the company's products. Harry, the Office Manager, was a nice man who'd worked for the company for many years and, at first, he wasn't too hard on me. However, my business levels were very low so, after a while, he allocated an inspector to me. The inspectors were high pressure sales whizz kids who were paid on a commission only basis and they worked with me on a Wednesday, my day off, to encourage me to make appointments for us to visit clients together and persuade them to take out new policies. I hated this part of the job and didn't make many appointments or back up the outrageous promises the inspectors made to potential customers about grossly exaggerated returns on their policies and pensions. Thankfully they could make more money working with the other agents, so they soon left me alone.

Left alone I quite enjoyed the job; it was a tough area, but the people who I dealt with were pleasant enough and a three-and-a-half-day week suited me fine. I had to generate new business and the company brought out a new contents insurance policy, which was a godsend to me. South Bank had more than its fair share of crime, particularly burglary, and most of my customers couldn't afford the premiums on standard contents insurance policies. The new policy which United Friendly introduced enabled them to have the premiums collected at their doorstep on a weekly or monthly basis, which fitted their budgets and lifestyles and was what people wanted, so I was happy to recommend it. Selling two or three of these policies a week kept Harry happy and I was happily working towards my personal target of working there for one year, and one year only.

However, in the early 1990s new, compulsory regulation was introduced for the insurance and financial sectors and Harry, who had been happily cruising towards retirement, was offered and accepted an early retirement package, as he didn't like the new rules and regulations. I was sorry to see him go; he had given me the opportunity to complete my one year with an insurance company and hadn't been a hard task master. In fact, as I was about to discover, he had been an easy task master. I had always thought that the company's name was totally inappropriate; there were about a dozen agents in the office and the company fostered a dog-eat-dog attitude, which meant that the agents were definitely not united and some of them were decidedly unfriendly. I found this attitude alien after so many years working as part of teams that all had the same objectives and helped each other achieve them and nicknamed the company 'Disunited and Unfriendly'.

Harry leaving came as a surprise and I was a bit apprehensive about the new boss, correctly so, as it turned out. He had been promoted from inspector and this was his first manager's position; he brought with him the traits I so disliked in the inspectors but, as manager, I couldn't argue with him. Talk about a new brush sweeping clean; I started to dread the weekly manager's meetings because it didn't matter how much new business was brought in, it was never enough. One by one he fell out with nearly all the agents in the office and things deteriorated; as the agents' morale suffered, so did their business levels.

I still had about three months to go to complete my one year's experience, so I just put my head down and bit my tongue. I had never been so unhappy in a job in my twenty-nine years of going to work and I used to go home and have a good moan to Chris. She'd strongly supported my decision to train to become a Financial Adviser and was a great support to me whilst I worked at United Friendly. She encouraged me to keep going; each day was another day nearer my target and, with her encouragement, I managed to complete fifty-four weeks at work and then resigned. I worked fifty-four weeks, as I'd had two weeks holiday and didn't want any slip-ups in my target of one complete year of experience.

My next step was the Financial Planning Certificate, which was in three modules with an exam at the end of each module. I had to buy the module material from the Chartered Insurance Institute and they held exams periodically. I chose not to work for a few months and studied at home, enrolling for each exam as soon as I could and travelling out of the area to take the exams. The first exam was in Sheffield and the next two in Newcastle. I found it quite frustrating waiting for the results after each exam before I could move on to the next module, but that was how it worked.

I passed my exams, thus gaining the necessary criteria to register with the Financial Intermediaries, Managers and Brokers Regulatory Association (FIMBRA), the self-regulatory body for the financial services industry in 1993. I now needed to get some proper work experience from an Independent Financial Adviser's company.

I went to see Dave Adbrook, who had advised me how to get thus far, and again he was a good help. He offered me a job on a self-employed basis. He had the agencies with all of the investment and insurance companies and agreed I could put my business through his company and he would take a share of the commission I earned. It was an ideal arrangement to get me started; I was covered by his professional indemnity policy, had a desk in his office, got secretarial help and had a place where clients could visit for appointments. Business was slow at the beginning but soon started to build up and Dave gave me a few leads to help me when he was busy. I didn't have any office expenses and we split my earnings on seventy-five/ twenty-five percent basis. If I brought the business into the office, I would pay Dave twenty-five percent of my earnings and, if it was an office lead, that is Dave's business, he would get seventy-five percent of what was earned. It worked well; I was self-employed, kept my own hours, didn't get any hassle off Dave and was building up my own business within his, whilst gaining valuable experience.

My philosophy for advising people was very simple. The initial client fact-find provided the necessary information and I discussed their objectives with them. I then put myself in their position asking myself questions such as, "What would I do for myself, what would I do for my children, what would I do for my Mother?" and applied the same principles. It worked, and later I passed this philosophy on to my new colleagues. Working within Dave's practice was working for both of us, so Dave expanded and, over the following couple of years, recruited three more experienced financial advisers.

When my son, Paul, was eighteen he joined Dave's company as a Trainee Financial Adviser; he was self-employed and in the early months I subsidised his income as he trained and studied for his exams. He had expressed a wish to become an IFA from the age of sixteen after he had taken his 'O' Levels. After getting Dave's agreement, I told him that a job was waiting for him, but the condition was that he continued to study for his 'A' Levels and his results had to be good enough to get him into University. I did this for two reasons; firstly, if he didn't like working in the financial industry, he would be able to carry on his education and, secondly, if he didn't have a target regarding his studies, he wouldn't have put the required effort into them.

I discovered the conditions were necessary as, in the year he was due to take his 'A' Levels, his sister, Hannah, 'shopped' him and told me he wasn't doing any studying; he had boasted that he didn't have to, as he had a job lined up. I had a little word in his ear and reminded him of our deal - if he didn't get good enough grades to go to university, he would be going back to college for another year. His response of "Aw come on Dad" cut no ice at all and he knew that I would carry out my threat. I'm pleased to say that Paul got slightly better grades in his 'A' Levels than his two older sisters, which he does remind them of. Having passed his exams, Paul received his Financial Planning Certificate on the 8th March 2002 and registered with the regulatory body, the Financial Services Authority, immediately.

Things were going well; I enjoyed the work and have always found it an extension of my interests and aptitudes. One of the other three advisers had left Dave's business, so now there were five IFAs, Dave, myself, Paul and two others, Steve Sanderson, who joined the company in 1996 and John Smith, who joined in 2001.

By September 2001 I was established in the business and Chris and I decided to take a month off work to visit my brother, Alan, and his family, who lived in Perth, Australia. Our first intercontinental flight was very memorable, for all the wrong reasons. We'd booked the flight months before and the day we flew was just ten days after the September eleven attacks. I've never liked air travel but, since the Piper disaster, my opinion of flying had diminished considerably and I liked it even less. I accept that I have to grit my teeth and get on with life, but I still take a deep breath and say a few prayers before and during flying and whilst landing. I can cope if it is a nice smooth flight but, if there is any turbulence, my macho attitude quickly goes out of the window and I am very pleased to have Chris sat next to me for reassurance and a hand to hold. On this occasion the plane was less than half empty, as lots of passengers had cancelled their flights following the terrorist attack on the Twin Towers in New York, so Chris and I enjoyed the comfort of a double window seat and a bank of four seats in the middle, which were great to sleep on. It was much the same coming back a month later, but the additional seating did nothing to diminish the fear of disaster lurking around the corner once again throughout the flights.

When we arrived home, Paul came around to see us very quickly bearing bad news. Terry Outterside, my best pal who had been such a support to me in the months following the Piper disaster, had collapsed whilst we were in Australia and had been diagnosed with an aggressive brain tumour. Typical of Terry's consideration for other people, he had ordered Paul not to tell me until I came home, so as not to spoil my holiday. I was very upset, as was everyone who knew Terry. He lived for another nine months; he had surgery followed by radiotherapy, but the prognosis was poor and turned out be very accurate.

He had his driving license taken off him and, as he physically recovered, we started playing squash together again; he loved it and was so grateful that I used to pick him up, play a session with him and then take him home and spend some time with him. He used to thank me profusely and I could not get it through to him that it was an absolute pleasure and I classed it a privilege to be able to do it. The games and meetings were the top priority in my diary; they were sacrosanct to me and something I looked forward to with tremendous pleasure.

I saw a lot of him whilst he was ill and two things in particular stick in my mind, both towards the end of his life when he was in the hospice. Chris and I went to see him one day and his wife, Margaret, was there with her friend. After a while the three ladies went out for a cuppa and left Terry and I chatting. As soon as the ladies left the room, Terry asked me to quickly give him a hand to the loo whilst they were gone. He got out of bed but couldn't support himself and I just managed to hold him up. We were stuck; I had hold of him, but I couldn't move him, he was far too heavy, and he couldn't move. It took all my strength to stop him from falling, I couldn't get him back on to the bed and the pull cord for the nurse was tantalisingly close, but just out of reach. We were stuck there for about ten minutes, which felt like a lifetime to me, until a nurse walked past the door and heard my shouts. What a telling off we both got, me from 'nurse' Chris and Terry by the hospice nurse and his wife Margaret, though more gently. Chris and Margaret both remind me of it now, but all I was doing was trying to help a pal. Apparently, my name is in the hospice incident log.

My other memory is when, on one of my visits to the hospice, my mobile phone rang; it doesn't ring often, as I'm not as attached to it as the younger generation are. I went outside to answer it and, when I came back into Terry's room, he asked, "Do you think it's safe using them? Did they have anything to do with what's happened to me?". We agreed that, for all the experts say they're safe now, that might change; after all the experts said smoking was safe during the last century. You can understand why we got on so well; Terry was as big a cynic as me, and I still miss him today.

16

TAKING OVER THE BUSINESS

In 2002 the dynamics in the business began to change but neither my colleagues nor I spotted the subtle changes. Dave had been attending night-school classes for a while to learn Spanish, then he had a one-to-one tutor, then he went to stay in rural Spain with his tutor where nobody spoke English. He owned a property in Tenerife and we put his interest in speaking Spanish down to this, even though his learning seemed a bit over the top for a couple of holidays a year. In 2003 we learnt why Dave wanted to be so proficient in Spanish; he was going to live in Spain and open a business there and was looking to exit Abrook Financial Management.

Steve, John, Paul and I had to make some quick decisions. We all worked together well and had the choice of Dave selling the business to an outsider, taking our clients to another IFA practice, or buying the business off Dave and continuing to run it ourselves. Dave offered a good deal to any or all of us on condition that we rented the premises off him and kept all the staff on, carrying on their years of service, terms and employment conditions. Unfortunately Steve and John didn't want to buy the business so I was faced with a dilemma: I didn't want all of the upheaval of moving and Paul was doing well in the business.

I was fifty-five years old at the time and was quite happy working three or four days a week on a self-employed basis with little job pressure. There was plenty of time to play golf and pursue my other interests. I wasn't looking for a challenge of this kind, yet circumstances presented the opportunity and I knew it was the right thing to do for myself, for Steve and John and especially for my son, Paul. I prayed long and hard about the decision and firmly believe that God helped and guided me, both in the decision to buy the business and as I've continued to seek to work ethically and honestly for my clients, colleagues and employees in the intervening years. Chris was very supportive and encouraged me to go ahead with the business, whilst also pointing out the practicalities of the decision and that I would need to start working full-time again, something I hadn't done for a lot of years. The golf had to take a back seat!

I spoke with John and Steve who both said that they would stay on and work for me and they've both been good to their word and are still working with me now. I renamed the business Acklam Financial Ltd. and tried to register the company with the Financial Services Authority (FSA) to secure the legal permissions to give advice and be regulated by their rules. We live in a bureaucratic world and they wouldn't register the business as it didn't have any professional indemnity insurance. I contacted the insurance brokers and they would not give me any professional indemnity cover as the company wasn't registered with the FSA. You couldn't make it up, but after much to-ing and fro-ing I got the permissions and the indemnity cover and the business was officially established on the 24th July 2003. Dave went off to live in Spain and the name at the front of the office changed. It wasn't my intention to take on this challenge at fifty-five years old, but I did and fifteen years later I'm still working at it.

The first week that I took the business over, one of the men that I played cricket with asked if he could have a self-employed role within the business. He was an Independent Financial Adviser registered with the FSA and, after agreeing a contract, he joined the company, meaning we now had five financial advisers. The company continued to grow and my lease with Dave had expired. He wanted to put the rent up, but we couldn't agree on a figure, so I continued to pay the current rent, but I was skating on thin ice as he could have given me six months' notice at any point. The office was a shop unit on a busy shopping precinct in Middlesbrough and I didn't want to move off the precinct leaving the premises empty, potentially to be rented by another firm of financial advisers.

In 2003 a client of mine who organised courses at one of our local Further Education centres asked me if I would be prepared to lecture for a year to students wishing to gain their Financial Planning Certificate. It was a challenge and I wasn't too sure about my level of competence as a teacher; the students were paying good money to attend college and I wanted to do the best I could for them. I bought the course tutor's study books and adapted them to my own style, quickly discovering that preparation is a big part of teaching, as I sought to make the very dry and boring content interesting and engaging. I quickly learnt that poor preparation meant poor performance, as you couldn't bluff it out for three hours in front of a class full of students, and I didn't want to bluff it out. I remembered the lousy teachers I had at school and the very good ones I had at night school, who really helped me and gave me another chance – here was I at night school helping to give other people another chance.

At the first class I was amazed to see about forty eager students, from very different backgrounds, all crammed into the classroom. After the first few weeks the numbers thinned out a bit and, at the start of the second term, having taken their first exam, the numbers reduced to about half. Slowly the numbers continued to dwindle and, by the end of the third and final term, there were about seven students who sat the final exam. For those with no knowledge or experience within the financial or insurance sectors the course was extremely difficult and all those who qualified worked within the financial sector. Looking back, I moaned about my job with United Friendly but I was glad of the experience I gained working there and the training they provided.

I enjoyed lecturing and helping people to gain their qualifications and the 'thank you' cards I got from students who passed their exams were a source of encouragement to me. One of my former students is now the Managing Director of a local company which is bigger than Acklam Financial. I taught from 2003 until 2005 when I had to stop due to pressure of work with the business. I'm pleased that I was given the opportunity to teach and the principles I learnt there, particularly about good preparation, stood me in good stead when I was later asked to give presentations about Piper Alpha.

My daughter, Hannah, who is a year older than Paul, had trained as a Podiatrist and had a small self-employed business that she was building up, but it was slow and a bit intermittent. She realised that Paul was earning a lot more than she was; the car he drove was a dead giveaway. She asked if she could enrol at my night class and see if she could gain the qualification and, if she did, would I give her a job? She knew the answer, as Chris and I have always treated the children the same. All credit to Hannah, she stuck it out and passed her exams. Having Hannah in the class kept me on my toes, as any mistakes were quickly pointed out to me in the car on the way home. As I stated earlier, it is a hard course if you haven't any work experience, but I suppose it helps if your Dad is the tutor and he helps you with your homework.

Hannah came to work for Acklam Financial Ltd as a trainee and, on the 11th March 2005, passed her Financial Planning Certificate and qualified as an IFA. Acklam Financial was developing into a family business and this became more so when Hannah married one of the other IFAs in the office, Steve Innocent. Hannah isn't as driven as Paul and I was looking for her in the office one day when the Office Manageress said that she had gone out. Asking her where she'd been upon her return, she nonchalantly replied, "Out on an appointment". On further enquiry she admitted that her appointment had been at the hairdressers, not the kind of appointment I expected in work time. On another occasion when she was out of the office again, her 'appointment' turned out to be at her French class. In exasperation I asked her to learn what the French was for "I must spend more time in the office".

One morning in 2008 at 3:30 am Steve Sanderson phoned to tell me that he'd received a phone call from one of his clients who was a policeman, to say that there was a major fire on the shopping precinct, where our office was situated. My thoughts immediately raced back to the fireball on Piper Alpha and my initial reaction was, "Not another fire". He was advised that, if we needed anything out of the office, we should get there quickly. When I arrived at the scene, the fire, which was in an Indian restaurant on the first floor of the precinct above three of the shops, was raging, the main road was blocked and there were four fire engines at the scene. The whole precinct had flat roofs which were covered in bitumen and felt, and the wind was blowing the fire towards the other shops and offices, including our office. The situation looked grim until the wind direction suddenly changed, and the flames were blown away from the precinct enabling the fire brigade to bring the fire under control. Our office and the remainder of the shops and offices survived. We breathed a sigh of relief and opened for business as usual the following morning. Once again, I'd got off lightly from a potentially serious fire situation.

The owner of the properties was not as fortunate, as the restaurant was completely gutted; the premises next door on the first floor and the first four ground floor shops had extensive fire and water damage. It was arson and the tenant from the restaurant went to jail; not only had he fallen behind with his rent, he'd set the building on fire to try to cover his tracks. I kept my eye on the site and contacted the owner to enquire about renting the refurbished upstairs property once it was completed. He agreed, obtained change of use for the premises and they were rebuilt as purpose built offices, which we moved into several months later. We had lovely new offices with twice the space in a prominent position on the main road.

Acklam Financial has grown considerably since 2003. There are now seven financial advisors on the FCA register, four mortgage advisors and eleven other staff employed in varying roles; the anticipated turnover for the business at the end of the current financial year is approximately two million pounds. Chris works part-time in the business doing mainly office and clerical work, though her first love is to ensure the offices are clean and tidy and an attractive place for clients to visit. At the age of seventy I still work three and a half days a week in the business. I enjoy my work and have a lot of loyal clients, so hope to continue to work, but gradually reduce my hours. If anybody had said that I would still be working in 2018 when I started twenty-six years ago, I would have laughed at them but none of us know where life will lead us. My work started as a hobby before it became my employment and I've never lost my interest in financial matters, so it will continue to be a hobby when I do eventually retire.

I've been able to use the knowledge I've gained within the financial industry in my service for the church I attend, and which supported me so well in the period of time following the Piper Apha disaster. I was the local Church Treasurer for thirteen years and have been a member of the National Church Finance Board for the past twelve years. I've been pleased to make a positive contribution and have helped to ensure that the church's finances are sound and that Pastors within the denomination have adequate employment protection and pension provision. I keep being reselected for the position, so others must think that I'm doing something correct.

The ethos of the business has always been to 'look after people' and, as we've grown, that hasn't changed and is what we strive to do. Over the years the financial services industry has changed considerably. When I registered as an Independent Financial Adviser in 1993 the regulator was FIMBRA. As regulation has become more proactive over the years the regulatory body changed to the Personal Investment Authority then the Financial Services Authority and is now the Financial Conduct Authority.

As regulation within the industry tightened, so did the qualifications required for registration. A new minimum qualification standard of a Level Four Diploma for Financial Advisers had to be achieved by the first of January 2013, regardless of age or experience. Once the exams had been passed you then had to apply for a Statement of Professional Suitability, which has to be renewed each year, following the completion of required continued professional development.

Many people of my age and experience complained to the regulator but they were insistent; either you passed the exams or, to quote Lord Sugar, "you're fired". I thought long and hard about retiring but was persuaded by Hannah and Paul to get the required qualification. The exam was in three parts, a multiple-choice exam on rules and regulations, a researched and referenced essay on a given financial subject and a four-hour written exam where you were given a case-study and had to write a suitability report for the client, by far the easiest part of the assessment and something we do for every client. At the age of sixty-five, having taken the entrance exams twenty years previously, I had to study and sit exams at a level I would never have expected to achieve. Yet I did and once again proved 'where there's a will there's a way'.

Looking back over my work life I can see how life has moved on and how circumstances have affected my attitudes and perspectives on life. Before the Piper Alpha disaster I was very driven and competitive, always wanting to succeed, and this has diminished. I still like to win; if you ask my brothers, Mike and Trevor, and Peter Fitzpatrick, who I play golf with on a Saturday, they will tell you I'm still competitive and like to win, but I accept defeat a lot better than I used to. I'm not driven in the way I used to be, and my business success has come almost by accident. I've worked hard because a lot of people's livelihoods depend upon the business, not because of a personal need to succeed. I was prepared to let the opportunity to buy the business pass me by, but took it on because I believe that is where God led me, encouraged by Chris.

17

LESSONS LEARNT

In the weeks leading up to the twentieth anniversary of the Piper Alpha disaster, BBC Scotland came down to Middlesbrough to interview me for a series of special features they were filming to mark the anniversary. The BBC ran five items from Monday to Friday in the week of the anniversary on Look North, their local news programme, which followed the 6 o'clock news. I featured in one of the programmes.

The following week I received a telephone call from the Safety Officer for Sabic on their North Tees plant, asking if I would be prepared to talk about my experiences on Piper Alpha at one of their safety meetings. I was very unsure about the value of talking about something that happened twenty years ago but agreed to go to meet him and his boss. I decided to give it a go and they agreed to pay me for the talk; getting paid to talk about the Piper Alpha disaster was a first, as I'd always happily talked to the press, radio and TV for nothing.

On the day of the talk I was given a safety helmet and taken to the plant where I was to give the talk. It felt surreal being back in that environment and it was the first time I'd worn a safety helmet for over twenty years. The Safety Officer warned me that I was likely to get a cool reception from the audience as, due to the company's shift pattern, the men were having to work days back that they 'owed' the company and they resented this. I was nervous enough about talking to an audience for the first time and even more apprehensive at the prospect of a cool reception from these experienced shift personnel.

One of the documentary films about the disaster was shown and then I recounted the events leading up to the explosions, how I escaped and my experience of watching the disaster unfold before my eyes from the Silver Pit. One of my Oxy colleagues, George Fowler, had previously worked for Sabic on the plant and, early on in my talk, one of the audience asked if I knew him. I did; George was a keen squash player and used to play with Terry and I when our shift patterns allowed. Unfortunately, George was on the day shift on the 6th July and was killed in the disaster.

The audience was very receptive to my talk and asked lots of questions and, when I'd finished, gave me a round of applause. As the Safety Office escorted me from the plant he remarked how surprised he was; that was the first time they'd ever given anyone a round of applause. I was invited back to give another five talks to the different shifts. After my initial nervousness, I grew in confidence and, as the audiences asked lots of pertinent questions, I included the points raised in future talks, so the content improved and became more relevant to the audiences. I was very glad of my teaching experience at night school ten years earlier and the lessons I'd learnt about preparation and presentation of material. A few weeks later I was invited to give a number of lectures to Sabic employees on the Wilton site, which in its heyday employed over thirteen thousand people.

I always end the talks by emphasising three things that went wrong on the night of the 6th July 1988. The Cullen Report made one hundred and six safety recommendations but these three very costly mistakes that were made really stick in my mind, and sometimes still keep me awake at night. If we had not made any one of these three errors the disaster wouldn't have happened the way it did. Mistakes were made with the three 'P's – permits, plant and personnel.

Firstly, the permits: there was a cold work permit issued (no. 23434) for the removal of PSV 504. This PSV (Pressure Safety Valve) was situated in C module on the 90ft level and was attached to condensate pump A, which was in the module below, i.e. the 68ft level. A second permit was also issued, a hot work permit, to allow the Oxy maintenance department to carry out PPM (planned preventative maintenance) on the pump. These two separate permits, which were for the same piece of equipment, should have been cross-referenced and whilst still active, that is the work not completed, should have been attached to each other. The permit that the maintenance department had would then have not been signed off, as the other permit was still live and required the pump to be isolated and reference to it would have shown that the safety valve was missing.

Secondly, the plant: the leak came from the blank flange fitted to the open pipe work where PSV 504 had been. If the blank flange hadn't leaked at the pipework where the safety valve had been removed, there wouldn't have been any gas to ignite. I accept that the condensate pump would have been running in a very unsafe manner, with no safety valve, but, in all my time on Piper, I had never known the pressure safety valve lift on either condensate pump.

Thirdly personnel: the shift handovers failed. Three people who were on the day shift should have handed over the fact that the PSV had been removed from condensate pump A and the three people who were on the night shift would then have known that the PSV was missing. Out of all the things that have bothered me over the last thirty years, this still bothers me the most. I can't believe that all six people involved didn't do it. I had worked with them for a lot of years and they were all very competent and conscientious people and it is so difficult to believe that all of them forgot to mention such an important thing. These things are written in the handover log and discussed at the handovers and, unlike some handovers onshore, where people were often in a hurry to get away, offshore the operators handed over in the control room and did it thoroughly. Unfortunately none of the logs were recovered, unlike permit no. 23434 which was retrieved from the accommodation wreckage months later when it was lifted from the bottom of the sea.

I have given well over one hundred lectures across the UK and have been invited abroad to speak, resulting in some memorable trips. I was invited to Calgary in Canada to give two lectures, one to plant operators and one to the Managing Director and his fellow directors. My flight to Canada was an experience for me, as the company paid for me to fly business class. It was the first time I'd travelled business class and, for a working-class boy from Thorntree, it was a memorable experience and one which has spoilt me for the future.

When my travel arrangements were being made, I asked if I could stay on an extra day to do some sight-seeing. The company were very agreeable and booked me into the hotel for an extra night and extended the itinerary. Having delivered both lectures successfully, I got up early on my last day and planned to go into Calgary to visit the famous Calgary Tower. When I walked out of the hotel I was greeted with thick freezing fog and a temperature of minus seven degrees; I couldn't even see the hotel car park. I hastily went back into the hotel and spent the day attending the safety training course with the men I had met the day before. I left the hotel at 7.00 pm to fly home; I hadn't seen much of Calgary, but I'd had a memorable trip.

My next trip abroad was to Stavanger in Norway; again to give just two lectures, one to the Managing Director and senior management and the other to the maintenance and production offshore supervisors. I enjoyed the trip; it was a short flight from Newcastle and thankfully the weather was good. I gave two lectures over three days, so enjoyed some leisure time exploring the city. On the day that I spoke to the offshore staff, the Senior Maintenance Engineer asked a question about how we handled the return of permits in the control room, which I explained.

Later that evening, over dinner, he commented that he had really enjoyed the lecture and found it very useful, as it corrected a misconception that he had, based on a documentary that he'd seen, about how we handled the permit system. I was appalled, and it made me wonder how many other people had the same misconception and thought that we were all totally incompetent. He agreed; his opinion for the last twenty-plus years had been that the systems they operated were a lot better than on the Piper and it was no wonder the accident had happened if our systems of control were as lax as the documentary had portrayed. The permit system was found wanting on the night of the 6th July and was one of three things which went wrong on disaster night, as explained earlier. There is a commentary on the five films and documentaries which have been made about Piper Alpha in Appendix 4, in which I refer in detail to the inaccurate portrayal of how we operated the permit system.

The third trip abroad took me to Perth, Australia. I flew business class again and this time I paid to take Chris with me and we extended the visit to make part of the trip a holiday. My older brother, Alan, and his wife, Val, live in Perth and it was really nice to see them and spend time with them. Whilst there, I gave four separate lectures for four different companies. One of the presentations was in the Perth Conference Centre and approximately four hundred people attended; this was a much bigger audience than I was used to and it was quite nerve-racking to see them all there. Thankfully, it was well received and, after the initial nervous start, the number of people present didn't make any difference; I just tell it as it was and is. It was a memorable trip from a personal point of view and both Chris and I enjoyed the visit. Chris has found the renewed interest and conversations about the disaster in the last ten years quite difficult, as it stirs up painful memories for her that that she would rather forget, so I was pleased we were able to go on this trip together.

As I said earlier, the talks started by request and I still do them on request. I'm a bit nervous when I start but I soon get into my stride and I don't get as upset as I did at the beginning, when the odd tear was shed. They've been very well received, and I have testimonials from people thanking me for correcting misconceptions and making them aware that the production teams on Piper Alpha were experienced and conscientious men who did their jobs diligently. Yet the accident still happened and could still happen again, as it did on a smaller scale on Deepwater Horizon.

Whilst working in the industry I'd attended numerous training events at the Spadeadam Training facility in Northumberland run by DNV-GL. It's an excellent facility for people employed in the oil, gas and chemical industries. The theoretical training is very good, and it's accompanied by live, practical demonstrations, such as fires and controlled explosions, which are outstanding and make the attendees very aware of the possibility of things going wrong and show the consequences graphically. In 2016 they opened a new conference and training building, opened by Lord Cullen, and I was invited to the grand opening. It was nice to meet him again and also Rod Sylvester Evans, the safety consultant who appeared in the documentary about Piper Alpha, 'Seconds from Disaster'. As we talked together, it didn't seem like twenty-seven years since I had last seen them.

One of the most common questions I'm asked in the talks is "Did you ever go back offshore?" and up until May 2013 the answer was always "No". The answer changed, because on 25th May and 30th May 2013 I made two trips to the Central gas platform in Morecambe Bay, which is operated by Centrica.

Mark McGee was the Safety Manager for the onshore and offshore facilities at Morecambe Bay. He contacted me out of the blue and asked if I would speak at one of his safety meetings. I did, and things followed a similar pattern to my presentations at other companies; one lecture became two, which became six or seven. It was Mark who asked me to attend and speak at a Centrica safety course at Spadeadam. I was given very specific travel instructions on how to get to Spadeadam, as the test and training facility is actually inside an RAF base in a very secluded area of Northumberland. I would never have found it otherwise, as I had to drive through 'No Through Road' and 'Strictly No Admittance to Unauthorised Personnel' signs. I had to produce my passport for ID, my car number plate was taken, and I was photographed; security was very tight.

However, back to Mark who I got on well with and who was a good help in advising me on my presentations. He phoned me early in 2013 and asked if I would consider, just consider, going on to the Central platform in Morecambe Bay, as he was planning some safety events to coincide with the twenty-fifth anniversary of the disaster. My immediate response was, "No chance!" and he agreed, but left it with me.

To cut a long story short, over the next few months my attitude softened and "No" became "I'll think about it" then "I might give it a try" and finally I agreed to go, on the basis that there was no pressure and I could call it off at any point. That included me getting to the point that, even after I had boarded the helicopter and was actually flying to the platform, I could call it all off and there would be no recriminations. Mark met all my conditions.

Before I was allowed to go offshore, I had to have a medical and pass my survival test again to comply with safety regulations. Even at sixty-five years old this part didn't bother me, as I'm an adequate swimmer and there is now a facility in Teesside, run by Falck, where you can take the half-day course. After the basic introduction I headed into the pool and was tested on swimming underwater, which was new to me, and the helicopter dunking, with and without a life jacket and using the little breather device in the life jacket. It was tougher than it used to be, but very practical and the staff at the facility were very helpful. Mark phoned me the next day to ask if I had passed and was very pleased that I had; I could imagine him putting another tick next to his list. I complimented him on the facility and how good the staff were, commenting that I had the pool to myself and the full quota of staff was very reassuring to me. He had a little laugh and said that they had been told who I was and warned to give me the kid glove treatment, as long as I passed the required standard.

Mark moved things forward and I was scheduled to go to visit the Morecambe Bay Central platform on the 23rd May 2013. I was very apprehensive and nervous about it all, but I was prepared to give it a try. Looking back, my determination to try to do it had grown the nearer that I got to the date and especially after successfully passing the survival course. I hoped that it would benefit me, and I have a good attitude to be loyal towards people who are loyal to me, so I didn't want to let Mark down.

It got to the 21st May and Mark and I spoke together about the trip and we both knew that there was one very important person who had to agree to the visit or it would be called off, and up to this point I had said nothing. I'd told Mark that unless I had total agreement from Christine, I would not do it. I had told Chris that I would be away on the evening of the 22nd May, returning the following evening. Chris still found the continued interest in the disaster after so long difficult to understand so I was wary of broaching a potential trip offshore with her. I explained that I'd been asked to give the presentation offshore and that the Central platform was about eight miles out in the Irish Sea, so it meant I would have to get on board a helicopter for the first time in twenty-five years to fly to the platform. Her response was totally unexpected, "Geoff, I think that you should go there tomorrow and get on that helicopter and slay a few more demons in your life." I phoned Mark and told him that I would be at Blackpool airport at check-in time for the flight.

I was very nervous, but I did it. I flew in a helicopter for the first time in twenty-five years. Fortunately for me, and for Centrica, considering the money that they had spent up to now, it was a lovely calm and bright sunny day. Things were very different from twenty-five years earlier. The survival suit, instead of being a strong, bright orange plastic bag with two arms and two legs and a space at the top for your head, came in a large variety of sizes and the staff giving out the suits made sure that it fitted you properly, to enable it to be as effective as possible, if needed.

For the first time in my life I was given a chaperone, who sat me in the middle of three seats and he sat next to the escape exit. Mark sat by himself in the row in front and we were the only three passengers onboard. Off we went, flying over Blackpool on a lovely sunny, windless day. I had prayed for perfect conditions and it couldn't have been better; had it been overcast or windy, I think that I would have 'bottled it' and gone back home.

There had been many changes since I last set foot on an offshore platform, most notably in the accommodation provision. Unlike the Piper platform, where the living accommodation was above the turbines and in the next module to the gas plant, the Morecambe Central platform was comprised of three adjoining structures, one for the drilling activities, one for the production facilities and one for the living accommodation and messing facilities. If only the Piper had a separate platform for accommodation and messing. If only? I understand that all new offshore facilities in UK waters do have a separate platform for accommodation.

I also travelled to the Morecambe Central platform on the 30th May 2013 and again the weather conditions were excellent and that was the last time I travelled in a helicopter. They always say, 'never say never' and I made the mistake of saying that before, but I doubt if I will ever fly in a helicopter again. I do fly in fixed wing planes as a necessary part of normal life, but I am not over keen on flying. Sadly Mark died shortly after my visits to Morecambe Bay; he was a considerable help to me in laying to rest a few more of the residual demons from the Piper Alpha and he was very passionate about his job and his role in ensuring a safe working environment.

I've made it to the end of this book and brought my story up to date. I wouldn't have got this far without the help and encouragement from the people named in the acknowledgment. I'm not a writer and have found this book difficult from a skills point of view, and even more difficult from an emotional point of view. I must confess to shedding a few tears whilst writing and remembering the sad events in my life.

Thirty years on from the Piper Alpha disaster I still consider myself very fortunate to have survived with only minor physical injuries. I count my blessings and appreciate the little things in life in a way I didn't before. I have been able to enjoy those things in life which many of us take for granted; watching and being part of my children growing up and having three lovely grandchildren to spend time with and enjoy. I'm very grateful to Christine and to the children for their love and support, especially during the darkest times in our lives. I thank God every day that I survived such a horrific disaster and I hope that my story will bring a measure of encouragement to others that, whatever we may face in life, there is always hope and daylight at the end of the tunnel.

Appendix 1

STATEMENT FROM G. BOLLANDS TO OCCIDENTAL MANAGEMENT FOLLOWING THE DISASTER

I started work in the Control Room about 17.10 hours on Tuesday 5th August 1988 and took over from John Slaymaker. He briefed me on what had been happening. Nothing unusual happened that night. I do not remember which condensate pump was running. I finished my shift at 05.15 hours on Wednesday 6th July 1988 and John Slaymaker took over from me in the Control Room.

I then went to bed in my room A1 in the Accommodation Module. I shared a room with John Brian Kirby, a Production Operator, also with Occidental, who was on the opposite shift to me.

About 14.00 hours that day (6th July 1988) I arose and about 17.15 hours I started my shift in the Control Room, taking over from Raymond Price. Raymond told me that line 2 metering lines were in operation with line 1, instead of lines 1 and 3 together – we had three lines for metering the oil we produced. It could be metered through any of the three lines and we metered it through two of the three, usually 1 and 3. I was told that there was a different well in test, which I think was P53, which was due to finish at 20.00 hours that evening. (This has no relevance to the explosion but shows the routine work ongoing in the Control Room.)

At that time the indicator board was showing that there was only 'B' condensate pump running. Normally we had both condensate pumps running but, as we were in Phase 1 operation, one pump was enough as we were not making so much condensate.

The new night shift came on about 17.15 hours. They were Bob Vernon, Erland Grieve, Bob Richards, Gordon Rennie and Sandy Bremner. There was nothing abnormal about anything in the Control Room.

About 19.00 hours Erland Grieve, Gas Conservation Operator (Phase 2) radioed me and asked me to relay a message to Bob Richards (Phase 1 Operator) to check something to do with the methanol injection points. I called Bob on the radio but he had already heard Erland speaking to me. I heard them speaking to each other and they sorted the problem out. I do not know any details of it.

After that I asked the 'oily water' lads, Gordon Rennie and Sandy Bremner, to put 2 fine water filters in commission and isolate 2 others. Bob Vernon said that the maintenance had finished with line 3 and to get Gordon and Sandy to check out and pressurise line 3 meter stream. I passed on this message to them to do it after 20.00 hours. (This also has no relevance to the explosion.).

At 20.00 hours I took a set of test and metering readings as routine. About this time I telephoned Mahmood Khan, the Chemist in the chemical laboratory, and asked him to take a sample of the water cut from line 3 meter stream at 22.00 hours.

We then had a coffee break in the Control Room. Every evening around 20.00 hours, sandwiches and cakes were brought down to the Control Room. We had coffee and tea making facilities in the Control Room and the people who were on shift came in when they were free, the Production Operators, one or two of the maintenance lads and the occasional Safety Officer.

Up until then I had been kept fairly busy without being rushed but everything had been quite normal and routine.

During the coffee break, about 20.15 hours, a U.V. detector indicated by audio and visual display that there was a flame in the 68ft level somewhere in the condensate area under 'C' Module.

I cancelled the audible alarm and accepted it (ie switched off the flashing light) and told Bob Richards who was in the Control Room. He informed me that there was a Welder down there and Bob Vernon said he had a permit. I had passed the message onto the Production Operator which was my responsibility. I know Bob Richards was quite happy with the situation.

I knew there was permission for hot work ongoing on the 68ft level for the Chanter riser. The permits which were in force were kept in boxes in the Control Room. The permits for hot work were in a red/pink colour and stood out in the box.

About 10 to 15 minutes after that I got a low gas alarm, again audio visually from the drill rig area. Erland or I accepted it on the main board (ie pressed the button on the main board to stop it flashing) and Erland went round to the back of the board to identify the individual detector which had been activated and pressed it to reset it. It reset and then almost immediately the same gas detector went off again at the front and again showing a low gas alarm.

Erland telephoned the drill floor for me and told them. I spoke to Robbie Carroll, the Safety Operator, and informed him. He left to investigate. He had a hand detector but returned about 15 minutes later and told me that there was no gas there, but I still could not reset the alarm. I then contacted John Wakefield, the Fire and Gas Instrument Technician, and informed him of the situation by telephone. He was working with John Cooper, a Contract Instrument Technician, who was assisting him.

About 21.00 hours, John Wakefield returned to the Control Room and informed me that it was a faulty gas head on the drill floor, which he believed was contaminated with diesel fumes. He was unable to reach it as he needed scaffolding, so he isolated it from the system. The low gas alarm remained lit on the board. I do not know why it remained lit after it had been isolated. (We did get the odd spurious alarms particularly with faulty detectors. We often got false alarms from C. Centrif. They were a bit of a nuisance but we always checked them out.)

In between times Eddie, the Diving Clerk who worked for Stena, had gone to Bob Vernon and asked for the pump status sheet. This sheet indicated which sea water intake pumps were on and which were off. I gave him the sheet and I signed it with him and kept a copy in the Control Room. The 3 source water pumps for water injection were on and the 2 utility electric pumps for sprinklers and deluge were on. As diving operations were going to be carried out that night the 2 diesel pumps which were a back-up for the electric pumps (sprinklers and deluge) were in the manual position. The diesel pumps could not be switched on or off from the Control Room but only by means of a switch situated beside the water pumps.

Every time the divers were in the water the diesels were changed to manual. The intakes for the diesel pumps were both together underneath 'D' Module.

After 21.00 hours I spoke to Sandy about getting line 3 going. He had put another well on test by this time but I do not know which one.

Mahmood telephoned me about taking the water sample figure from line 3 but I told him to forget about taking a water cut at 22.00 hours as the job had not been done.

I then carried on with my paperwork.

About 21.30 hours I left the Control Room, leaving Bob Vernon there, and went to the Maintenance Clerk's office to telephone my wife. Nothing unusual had happened up to that time. At 21.40 hours I returned to the Control Room and remained there with Bob Vernon.

About 21.50 hours the 'B' condensate pump alarm tripped, alarming audio and visually, the red light went out and the amber light started flashing. I pressed the button to cancel the audio signal and stop the amber light flashing and I contacted Bob Richards on the radio and told him that the pump had tripped.

Bob Vernon left the Control Room to go and help him, having told me that 'A' condensate pump was out of commission for maintenance. Although he did not say it, I am sure he went to the condensate pump.

I knew before this time that 'A' condensate pump was not going as the light was showing amber and not red. I was aware that this pump was with maintenance and that Willie Young had a permit to work on this machine. I did not know what was wrong with the pump.

Two or three minutes later a J.C.P. alarm (I do not know the number) activated audio and visually (part of the main production panel). This alarm told me there was an alarm on the J.C.P. panel (ie the panel beside the 'A' condensate machine on the 68ft level). I assumed it to be the condensate drum (C701) high level alarm. I accepted it and told Bob Richards by radio. He was at the condensate pump and would have seen it on the panel at the condensate pump.

Two or three minutes later, Bob Vernon ran back into the Control Room and said the pump, ie 'B' condensate pump, would not restart. He grabbed the permit from the box in the Control Room that was out for 'A' pump which was shut for instrument plant maintenance and he tannoyed for Alex Clark, the Maintenance Leadhand. I knew Bob had to sign the permit off before he could get the machine going. He had to sign the permit and 2 requests for electrical de-isolation tags. I could see 2 bright red tags (isolation tags) attached to the permit.

I asked Bob Vernon if the 'recips', ie the reciprocating compressors 'A' and 'B' were unloaded (gas being flared off) as we had just had a high level alarm and he said, yes they were. I assumed that Bob Richards would have unloaded them (this was done by flicking 5 switches on each machine) but I just wanted to check with Bob Vernon to make doubly sure. Because the gas was being flared off the plant was not in any danger from too much condensate. Condensate was still coming through from 'C'-202 but only in negligible amounts. It produced approximately 35% and 65% came from the recips.

The phone rang almost immediately after the tannoy and I heard Bob speaking to someone who was obviously Alex Clark. He told him he wanted 'A' pump into commission immediately.

Alex Clark came into the Control Room about 2 minutes later to sign the tags. Bob was still in the Control Room. Bob would have requested de-isolation and Alex would do as requested.

Almost immediately 2 of the 3 centrifugal compressor alarms tripped. I cannot now remember if it was 'A' and 'B' or 'B' and 'C'. I do not know what caused it. There are about 25 to 30 different trips on these machines. They are very sensitive machines and often tripped. The centrifugal compressors are at the east end of Module 'C' and when 2 tripped that left only one in operation. I had one centrifugal compressor running, 'A' or 'C', 2 reciprocating compressors running but unloaded and no condensate pumps.

Up to this time the situation did not worry me because we had experienced it before on numerous occasions. Normally we got one condensate pump going, loaded one of the recips and then started the 2 centrifs. It was not often that we had no condensate pumps going but we had taken the appropriate action and there was nothing to worry about for the moment. Everything was under control and what was necessary to be done was being done.

Alex Clark then tannoyed for James Savage, the day-shift Electrician, who had been working over until 22.00 hours. I thought at the time it would be unlikely if he could get him as it was minutes before 22.00 hours and he would be off duty.

Jim Savage then telephoned after a second tannoy message went out and I gathered he was in the Accommodation Module. Alex Clark then tried to contact the shift Electricians, John Hackett and Eddie Crowden.

Things then happened very quickly. I received the first gas alarm, audio visual. It was 'C' centrif – low gas. I accepted it and called Bob Richards on the radio and informed him that I had a low gas alarm in the centrifugal area. Then about a minute later, in very quick succession, I got 2 low gas alarms. It was the other 2 centrifs so I had the 3 of them up. They were audio visual alarms and, as I accepted them (switched off the audible alarms), the other centrif tripped so I had none. My first thought was that we would have no gas for the turbines and I was thinking that I would have to switch the John Brown on to diesel to keep power and tell Bob to open Valve 2 when he got the chance. (Valve 2 would return fuel gas from the Claymore line.)

As I was thinking that, trying to get him on the radio and also silence the gas alarm, I got a fourth low gas alarm (the fourth low gas alarm was above the others on the panel and I think it was east Module 'C' but I am not entirely sure.)

At the same time a high gas alarm on the centrif ('A', 'B' or 'C' – I cannot remember which) came up. I had my hand out to stop the audible alarm but, before I had time to do that, there was a sudden explosion from the south side of the Control Room and I was flung northwards across the room.

When I came to and started picking myself up, I noticed that the dark emergency lighting was on. I was conscious that my right hip was painful, but I had crawled back to the main panel and pressed the main shutdown button to shut down everything on the rig. By this time the room was filling with grey smoke which was rolling towards me/ above me.

I cannot say if any indicator lamps were showing on the control board. I am not conscious of seeing any lights on the control board and I would think that, had there been any, I would have noticed them.

I saw that Alex Clark had been flung in the same direction and had hit the bulkhead beside the double doors of the room. He was dazed and had been hit by some machinery. I picked him up. Ian Ferguson, one of the

Fitters, came into the Control Room and helped me with Alex Clark and we all went out of the Control Room and westwards down the steps. There was thick black smoke coming from the explosion area in 'B' Module and being blown in a north-easterly direction across the rig. It totally enveloped the north side of the rig and I could not see lifeboat number 4 or 5. Due to the wind direction the north-west corner of the platform was clear of smoke.

I saw a lot of flames coming round the crane pedestal from the south at 'B' Module.

At the foot of the stairs which led to the Control Room, we met Bob Vernon, Robbie Carroll, Erland Grieve and Willie Young, who asked what had happened. I was concerned that the platform alert had not gone off. Robbie Carroll broke the glass in a manual alarm, but nothing happened. Bob McGregor broke the halon alarm which floods the Control Room, but I do not know if this worked. We stood and talked about the situation. We knew the fire pumps were on manual and this caused us a lot of concern. We were also worried about the fact that the platform alert had not gone off. This alert would have told everyone to go to their emergency stations, ie boats or emergency duties. Even if the electric failed it should have gone off as there was a back-up system which was battery powered. The fire and gas panel was damaged in the explosion.

Bob Vernon and Robbie Carroll both put on breathing apparatus and were about to go and try and switch on the fire pumps when Erland Grieve and Willie Young said that my thumb was bleeding. I then noticed that my thumb was in fact bleeding badly and I had it bandaged with a handkerchief. A number of other men, including the Stena lads, came up from the 68ft level and then I realised that Bob and Robbie had left but I did not know which way they went.

Between 5 and 10 minutes after the first blast, there was another explosion which I think came from 'C' Module and we decided it was time to move. There was nothing we could do because there was no water and we were being showered with sparks. I could hardly walk because of my hip and I knew it was time to try and make an escape. Had we been able to go up the stairs we would have gone to our muster point/ emergency duty station, but the stairs were enveloped in thick black smoke and the only way we could move was down.

We all moved downstairs to the 68ft level. The corner was still clear of smoke. There was a life box with jackets in it and these were distributed, and I got one and put it on. Some men asked how to get to the 20ft level but I told them to forget about that as the only stairs down were beside the condensate pumps and I knew it was impossible to go that way because of the smoke. During this time there were other minor explosions. I wanted to get down as low as possible, so I went down a ladder to a small platform which is used for a fog warning beacon. Someone had thrown a knotted rope over the side and men were starting to climb down the rope.

I was not very happy about going down the rope but there was no alternative, so I gritted my teeth and got on with it. It was difficult because of my thumb and my life jacket kept snagging on the rope. Ian Ferguson and Alex Clark had come down to the platform with me and Ian Ferguson was behind me. Alex Clark was still in a dazed condition and, when we got to the foot of the rope, we had to pass him across us. Two Stena lads helped us on to the 20ft level. We then walked along to B4 and waited for the Zodiac to return. As I had been climbing down the rope I saw a Zodiac boat taking a boat load of men to the Sliver Pit. The Zodiac returned and we climbed down into it. When there were about 10 – 12 people in it started back for the Silver Pit. While we had been waiting for the boat, there were a number of smaller explosions and hot sparks were falling from above, but we were getting protection from the floor above us.

When we were about 100 yards away from the platform I looked back and saw one lad fall from the rope and hit a stanchion. I then saw the rig engulfed in a fireball explosion and could only guess that the 'JT Flashdrum' had exploded. The heat was tremendous and the rig was burning completely.

We reached the Silver Pit and I got hold of the scramble nets. I could not get myself up but others onboard pulled me up. I think everyone on the Silver Pit did a very good job. There should perhaps have been better qualified medical staff onboard, but I am not criticising the chap who acted as a medic. He did all he could.

When I got onto the Silver Pit I had difficulty in walking. My thumb would not stop bleeding and it was bandaged again. After a full night on the Silver Pit I was transferred to the Tharos by helicopter where my thumb was re-dressed and my hip examined. I was taken to Aberdeen Royal Infirmary where I had a few stitches in my thumb. My hip was severely bruised. I had a puncture wound on the bone but was allowed home.

Physically I am well recovered apart from a little pain in my hip, but I am still on the sick list. I have difficulty in sleeping and I would not go back offshore again.

NOTE: I think the cause of the explosion could have been a leak from the condensate pump. This would fit in with the gas alarms which were at the east end of Module 'C'.

I did not know that PSV 504, the pressure relief valve for 'A' condensate injection pump, had been removed and was in the Score workshop on the evening of 6th July 1988. No-one told me in handover, but I would not have expected to be told. It was not my province.

The instrument lads work under a separate permit, a copy of which would have been in the Control Room if the work was ongoing. If work was stopped (even because of a shift change) the permit would have been suspended, ie signed off and put in the Safety Office.

There was only one permit in the Control Room and that showed the pump was isolated and electrically isolated. (If Score were working on the pump, both suction and discharge SDV would have been closed and the machine depressurised and vented – for an instrument PM just the valves would have been shut.) There was a box on the permit for any other ongoing work to be stated but this was not filled in.

Peter Grant was the Gas Plant Operator during the day and Joe Lynch was the Lead Operator until 10.00 am, when he went off duty to go onshore. Harry Flook, the stand-in Lead Operator, or Joe Lynch would have signed the permit to remove the valve. Joe would tell Harry what was being done, who would in turn tell Bob Vernon when he came on duty.

The person going off duty would inform the person coming on duty of all the work that was ongoing and anything of importance that had happened during the last shift. This would take anything between 2 and 10 minutes depending upon how busy the shift had been. Everything that had been done would have been noted in the log book and the person coming on duty would read the log.

There was a G.O.V. at the intake and output of 'B' condensate injection pump but there was no valve between the pump and the PSV.

If the Production operators, ie Bob Vernon, Bob Richards and Erland Grieve, thought they were going to start the pumps they could have opened the valves on either side of the pump, preparatory to having it electronically connected. Either Bob Richards, the Gas Plant Operator, or Bob Vernon, the Lead Operator, could have done this. If the valves were opened the condensate would come into the pump under pressure – 600 psi. If the PSV had been removed and replaced by a blank flange which was not pressure tested, the condensate could escape. When condensate is under pressure it is liquid but when the pressure is reduced to atmospheric pressure the volume is increased to approximately 500 to 1,000 fold. The gas would fill the area in Module 'C' and activate the alarms.

Appendix 2

TRIBUTE TO THE MEN WHO DIED

It is now thirty years since the disaster and I can still remember it as if it all happened yesterday. As the families and friends of the deceased reflect on it, their memories will be as vivid as mine; they have my sympathy and I salute my former colleagues who died.

Some of them I knew very well, others just to say 'hello' to and some I didn't know but I remember all of the men who died and herewith list them as a mark of my respect to them and their families. Lest we forget. I will not.

***

Robert McIntosh Adams, Rigger
George Alexander J Anderson, Baker
Ian Geddes Anderson, Dual Service Operator
John Anderson, Catering Manager
Mark David Ashton, Trainee Technician/Cleaner
Wilson Crawford A Bain, Valve Technician
Barry Charles Barber, Diving Consultant
Craig Alexander Barclay, Welder
Alan Barr, Electrical Technician
Brian Philip Batchelor, Seaman
Amabile Alexander Borg, Non-destructive Tester

Hugh Wallace Brackenridge, Roustabout
Alexander Ross Colvin Bremner, Production Operator
Eric Roland Paul Brianchon, Technician
Hugh Briston, Scaffolder
Henry Brown, Welder
Stephen Brown, Assistant Chef/Baker
Gordon Craib Bruce, Helicopter Landing Officer
James Bruce, Logger
Carl William Busse, Directional Drilling Supervisor
David Campbell, Cleaner
David Allen Campbell, Scaffolder
Alexander Watt Cargill, Electrician
Robert Carroll, Safety Operator
Alan Carter, Lead Production Operator
Robert Cleland, Derrickman
Stephen Colin Cole, Radio Officer
Hugh Connor, Instrument Technician/Lecturer
John Edward Sherry Cooke, Plater
John Thomas Cooper, Instrument Technician
William Nunn Coutts, Chef
William John Cowie, Steward
Michael John Cox, Scaffolder
Alan Irvin Craddock, Drilling Supervisor
Edward John Crowden, Electrical Technician
Bernard Curtis, Deputy Production Superintendent
Jose Hipolito Da Silva, Steward
John Stephen Dawson, Telecom Engineer
Eric Deverell, Production Clerk
Alexander Duncan, Steward
Charles Edward Duncan, Floorman
Eric Duncan, Drilling Materials Man
John Duncan, Engineer
Thomas Irvine Duncan, Roustabout
William David Duncan, Crane Operator
David Alan Ellis, Steward
Douglas Newlands Findlay, Supervisor Mechanic

Harold Edward George Flook, Production Operator
George Fowler, Electrical Technician
Alexander Park Frew, Plater
Samuel Queen Gallacher, Pipe Fitter
Miguel Galvez-Estevez, Assistant Chef
Ernest Gibson, Mud Engineer
Albert Stuart Gill, Roustabout
Ian Gillanders, Instrument Pipe Fitter
Kevin Barry Gilligan, Steward
Shaun Glendinning, Painter
John Edward Thomas Goldthorp, Motorman
Stephen Robert Goodwin, Geologist
James Edward Gray Gordon, Floorman
David Lee Gorman, Safety Operator
Kenneth Graham, Mechanical Technician
Peter John Grant, Production Operator
Cyril James Gray, Safety Operator
Harold Eugene Joseph Green, Rigger
Michael John Groves, Production Operator
John Hackett, Electrical Technician
Ian Hay, Steward
Thomas Albert Hayes, Rigging Supervisor
James Heggie, Production Services Superintendent
David William Henderson, Lead Floorman
Philip Robert Houston, Geologist
Duncan Jennings, Geologist
Jeffrey Grant Jones, Assistant Driller
Christopher Kavanagh, Plater
William Howat Kelly, Electrical Technician
Ian Killington, Steward
John Brian Kirby, Production Operator
Stuart Gordon Charles Knox, Roustabout
Alexander Rodger Laing, Steward
Terence Michael Largue, Scaffolder
Graham Lawrie, Roustabout
Findlay Wallace Leggat, Scaffolder

Brian Lithgow, Photographic Technician
Robert Rodger Littlejohn, Pipe Fitter
Martin George Longstaffe, Logger
William Raymond Mahoney, Steward
John Morrison Martin, Rigger
Sidney Ian McBoyle, Motorman
Robert Borland McCall, Chief Electrician
James McCulloch, HVAC Technician
Alistair James McDonald, Mechanical Technician
Alexander McElwee, Plater
Thomas O'Neil McEwan, Electrical Chargehand
William George McGregor, Leading Steward
Frederick Thomas Summers McGurk, Rigger
William Hugh McIntosh, Floorman
Gordon McKay, Valve Technician
Charles Edward McLaughlin, Electrician
Neil Stuart Ross McLeod, Quality Assurance Inspector
Francis McPake, Steel Erector/Rigger
David Allison McWhinnie, Production Operator
Dugald McLean McWilliams, Welder
Carl Mearns, Rigger
Derek Klement Michael Millar, Supervisor
Alan David Miller, Industrial Chemist
Frank Miller, Scaffolder
John Hector Molloy, Engineer
Leslie James Morris, Platform Superintendent
Bruce Alexander Ferguson Munro, Floorman
George Fagan Murray, Steward
James Cowie Niven, Roustabout
Graham Sim Noble, Materials Man
Michael O'Shea, Electrician
Robert Rennie Pearston, Mechanic
Ian Piper, Motorman
Wasyl Pochrybniak, Lead Roustabout
Raymond Leslie Price, Production Operator
Neil Pyman, Engineer

Terence Stephen Quinn, Service Engineer
William Wallace Raeburn, Maintenance Controller
Donald Reid, Chargehand Engineer
Robert Welsh Reid, Roustabout
Gordon MacAlonan Rennie, Process Operator
Robert Miller Richard, Production Operator
Alan Riddoch, Steward
Adrian Peter Roberts, Roughneck
Alexander James Robertson, Lead Production Technician
Donald Nicholson Robertson, Mechanical Technician
Gary Ross, Roustabout
Michael Hector Ryan, Roustabout
Stanley Sangster, Foreman Scaffolder
James John Dearn Savage, Electrical Technician
Michael Hugh Brodie Scorgie, Lead Foreman
William Alexander Scorgie, Pipe Fitter
John Francis Scott, Scaffolder
Colin Denis Seaton, Offshore Installation Manager
Robert Hendry Selbie, Turbo Drill Engineer
Michael Jeffrey Serink, Logger
Michael Bernard Short, Foreman Rigger
Richard Valentine Skinner, Assistant Driller
William Hamilton Smith, Maintenance Lead Hand
James Speirs, Mechanical Technician
Kenneth Stuart Stephenson, Rigger
Thomas Cunningham Boswell Stirling, Cleaner
Malcolm John Storey, Seaman
James Campbell Stott, Plumber
Jurgen Tilo Stwerka, Research Chemist
Stuart Douglas Sutherland, Student/Cleaner
Terrence John Sutton, Mechanical Fitter
Alexander Ronald Taylor, Roustabout
Alistair Adam Thompson, Telecom Engineer
Robert Argo Vernon, Production Operator
John Edward Wakefield, Instrument Technician
Michael Andrew Walker, Technician

Bryan Thomas Ward, Rigger
Gareth Hopson Watkin, Offshore Medical Attendant
Francis John Watson, Head Chef
Alexander Whibley, Roustabout
Kevan Dennis White, Maintenance Supervisor
Robert Whiteley, Roustabout
Graham Gill Whyte, Aerial Rigger
James Gilbert Whyte, Aerial Rigger
Alan Wicks, Safety Supervisor
Paul Charles Ferguson Williamson, Floorman
David Wiser, Survey Technician
John Richard Woodcock, Technical Clerk

Appendix 3

LIST OF SURVIVORS

Herewith a list of all of us who were fortunate to survive the events of 6th July 1988. Sadly, some of my former colleagues on this list are no longer with us.

***

Edward Amaira	Keith Cunningham
Robert Ballantyne	Iain Duguid
John Barr	Derek Ellington
William Barron	David Elliott
Geoffrey Bollands	Ian Ferguson
Michael Bradley	Ian Fowler
Fred Busby	Barry Goodwin
Harry Calder	Erland Grieve
Robert Carey	John Gutteridge
Andrew Carroll	Derek Hill
Neil Cassidy	Brian Jackson
Alexander Clark	Michael Jennings
William Clayton	Mahmood Khan
Richard Common	David Kinrade
James Craig	Charles Lamb

David Lambert

Ian Letham

Willian Lobban

Alastair MacKay

Stanley MacLeod

James McDonald

Robert McGregor

Ian McKenzie

Joseph Meanen

John Menzies

Stephen Middleton

Harold Miller

Andrew Mochan

Dean Naylor

Christopher Niven

Gareth Parry-Davies

Robert Paterson

Anthony Payne

Adrian Powell

Edwin Punchard

Steven Rae

Noel Ralph

Alexander Rankin

Mark Reid

James Russell

Anthony Sinnet

Vincent Swales

Donald Thompson

Roy Thompson

Joseph Wells

Alexander Wood

John Wood

William Young

Appendix 4

PIPER ALPHA FILMS AND DOCUMENTARIES, A COMMENTARY

There have been five documentary films made about the Piper Alpha disaster. The films portray the disaster with varying degrees of accuracy and some have contributed to creating the misconceptions which I have had to address in my presentations. In the commentary below, I seek to address those misconceptions from my personal experience and perspective.

PIPER ALPHA: SPIRAL TO DISASTER (1997) BBC, DISASTER SERIES 1, EPISODE 1

The BBC documentary 'Spiral to Disaster' was first shown on 7th January 1997. The portrayal of the events leading up to the disaster is inaccurate and does not portray the safety systems which were in place. One particular inaccuracy, which I have had to correct in several presentations, most notably on my visit to Norway when the Production Engineer decided to re-examine the integrity of their systems after learning the truth, is a dramatic portrayal of the permit system.

The film shows a worker on the platform entering the control room with a permit in his hand; he stands at the desk whilst, at the other end of the control room, the Control Room Operator and two other Oxy personnel totally ignore him and carry on talking as if he wasn't there. The contractor eventually gets sick of waiting and being ignored, picks a pen up, scribbles his name on the permit, throws it on the desk and, with a shrug of his shoulders, walks out.

This isn't how the permit system was administered and is insulting to the Production Supervisors who worked on Piper Alpha and sought to administer the systems rigorously. A contractor who had a 'live' permit to work would return to the control room at the end of their shift, or upon completion of the work, with their copy of the permit. The Shift Supervisor would retrieve the original from the control room and attach it to the copy. They would both then sign the permit off, as work completed or suspend the permit to be reactivated at a later time or date, and both copies would be returned to the safety office.

There are numerous other inaccuracies in the film, rendering it a factually inaccurate account of the disaster rather than a factual documentary.

SECONDS FROM DISASTER: EXPLOSION IN THE NORTH SEA (2004) NATIONAL GEOGRAPHIC CHANNEL, SERIES 1, EPISODE 10

'Seconds from Disaster' is much more factually accurate and has a very high visual impact. It is a good film and is worth watching. It features dramatic pictures of the giant fireball(s) and every time I see it, I realise how close I was to being caught by the first one and think about the poor men who were caught and trapped by them.

It has a few inaccuracies, the main one being the type of condensate pumps which are depicted in the film. In one of my presentations I was explaining that the pumps often tripped and, from an equipment point of view were the platform's 'Achilles heel', as we only had two pumps and in normal operating conditions we needed both of them. All the other pumps and compressors had stand-by equipment, if needed. The film states that "The condensate pumps had tripped and production crew were all feeling the pressure as the whole production facilities would soon shut down". I was contradicting this statement as it wasn't true, the worst that would have had to happen is that we would have to stop making condensate, i.e. flare the gas.

There was a Mechanical Engineer in the audience who queried why we had so much trouble with the type of pumps shown in the film, as they were usually very reliable. He was correct, the centrifugal pumps of the type that were shown in the film are very reliable, but the condensate injection pumps that we had on Piper were nothing like the ones shown. The Piper pumps were large, piston driven, reciprocating pumps which were always tripping. He was aware of the type of pump that I described and was pleased to have his misconception corrected. It illustrated again the importance of the information shown in documentaries being factually accurate.

PIPER ALPHA: FIRE IN THE NIGHT (2013) BBC SCOTLAND

'Fire in the Night' is a good film, which is based on the book written by Steve McGinty.[7] The film is more accurate in its portrayal of events than the previous two, as Stephen's book is accurate and is based on a considerable amount of research. In addition to the events surrounding the disaster, the film features a number of survivors and how they have coped in the intervening years.

WHAT CAUSED THE GIANT PIPER ALPHA OIL RIG EXPLOSION? (2017) SMITHSONIAN CHANNEL: MAKE IT OUT ALIVE – OIL RIG EXPLOSION

The Smithsonian Institution, which was originally established by an Englishman 'for the increase and diffusion of knowledge', is a group of museums and research centres administered by the Government of the United States. 'What caused the Giant Piper Alpha Oil Rig Explosion' is a

---

7 McGinty, Stephen. (2008) Fire in the Night: The Piper Alpha Disaster. London: Macmillan

short film depicting the disaster which was first shown on the Smithsonian channel on 5th November 2017. It was obviously made for an American audience as it has a distinct American bias and isn't as good as 'Seconds from Disaster' or 'Fire in the Night'.

JAMES NESBITT: DISASTERS THAT CHANGED BRITAIN (2018) HISTORY CHANNEL

This documentary was shown on 2nd April 2018. The History Channel previewed the series: *"Presented by award-winning actor James Nesbitt, the original six-part series unpicks the events that led to the most devastating disasters of the past 60 years. The unique documentary shines a spotlight on the human cost of the tragedies while seeking to explain the wider political, cultural and institutional context that contributed to them – and looks at the changes made in the wake of each disaster. The series asks why warning signs were often ignored and how seemingly innocuous decisions – sometimes decades before – contributed to the events that changed post-war Britain forever."*

I watched this with very mixed emotions. I get so frustrated about the emphasis on the drama/emotional aspect of the disaster and the disregard for the accuracy of the actual facts. For example, they kept calling me a 'manager'. I was a production operator. They completely blurred the very important points about permits and handovers. They gave the impression that the platform was ready to fall into the sea without the help of an explosion.

All credit to the daughters of Hugh Briston who both spoke so well about their Dad and their experiences. I couldn't help reflecting on how it could have been my two daughters speaking about their Dad.

Watching this programme has not changed my mind. The two most accurate programmes to watch are; 'Seconds from Disaster' and 'Fire in the Night'.